$12-50

Old Catholics and Anglicans
1931–1981

Old Catholics and Anglicans

1931–1981

*To Commemorate the Fiftieth
Anniversary of Intercommunion*

EDITED BY
GORDON HUELIN

OXFORD UNIVERSITY PRESS
1983

Oxford University Press, Walton Street, Oxford OX2 6DP

London Glasgow New York Toronto
Delhi Bombay Calcutta Madras Karachi
Kuala Lumpur Singapore Hong Kong Tokyo
Nairobi Dar es Salaam Cape Town
Melbourne Auckland
and associates in
Beirut Berlin Ibadan Mexico City Nicosia

Oxford is a trade mark of Oxford University Press

Published in the United States by
Oxford University Press, New York

British Library Cataloguing in Publication Data
Old Catholics and Anglicans 1931–81.
1. Old Catholic Church
I. Huelin. Gordon
284'.8 BX4765
ISBN 0-19-920129-3

Typeset by Oxford Verbatim Limited
and printed in Great Britain
at the University Press, Oxford
by Eric Buckley
Printer to the University

Foreword

JOHN SATTERTHWAITE

For many people, the Old Catholic Churches are unknown, but although they are small in number, they have an ecclesial importance which far outweighs their numerical strength. As it is now fifty years since the Church of England through its Convocations of Canterbury and York, entered into full communion with the Church of Utrecht, and its sister Old Catholic Churches, it seems appropriate that a book such as this should appear and give a wider understanding of the family of Catholic Christendom and of its ethos which has been hitherto largely unknown or ignored.

Although there had been many endeavours in the Church of England and elsewhere in the provinces of the Anglican Communion to promote reunion since the divisions caused in the west from the time of the Reformation, the Bonn Agreement of 1931 establishing full communion between the Anglican and Old Catholic Churches was the first significant accomplishment made by the Church of England to this end. Many have looked upon the Agreement as a model for unity schemes in the future, for churches of the Apostolic tradition involving episcopal government. By this Agreement each Church recognized the catholicity and independence of the other. Each church agreed to admit members of the other church fully to its sacramental life. It was agreed that the full communion established between the two churches did not require either church to accept all the doctrinal opinions, or the liturgical practices of the other, even though each church believed the other to hold all the essentials of the Catholic faith.

From the middle of the nineteenth century, at the time of the Oxford Movement, when J. M. Neale wrote about the so-called Jansenist Church of Holland his readers in England and elsewhere came to know something of the small church in The Netherlands which had then struggled for its existence well over a century. The problems created by the first Vatican Council of 1870 resulted in the break-away from Rome of the other Old Catholic Churches in Germany, Switzerland and Austria, but these have mostly been hidden away in the course of the past century.

In the religious upheavals of the sixteenth and seventeenth centuries the Church of Utrecht went through a time of fierce testing and trial. Philip II of Spain had made Utrecht an Archbishopric with five suffragan sees, but this did not stem the rise of Calvinism in the Spanish Netherlands. During the eighty years' war which ensued, the Church of Utrecht had to struggle for its rights, not only with the Papacy, but also against the fierce aggression of local Protestant Reformers. Even so, the Church of Utrecht continued faithfully its apostolic witness to the Catholic faith. When the Government of the United Provinces proscribed all Catholic worship at the end of the sixteenth century, the Church of Utrecht had to go into hiding, but it was prepared to face persecution and continue its ministrations as an underground church. Any visitor to Amsterdam, and other Dutch cities today can still see the remaining 'hidden churches' with their poignant evocation of former religious intolerance.

On the Catholic front, the Church of Utrecht had an equally fierce struggle through the intrigues of the Jesuit Order which sought control of the Church after accusing it of Jansenism, and which tried to get The Netherlands established as its own 'Missionary Territory'. When Archbishop Vosmeer was consecrated for Utrecht at the beginning of the seventeenth century he wrote that 'the inconvenience caused by the Protestants is less than the affliction originated by the Jesuits'. The struggle with the Jesuits was greatly intensified after the death of Bishop van Neercassel in 1686, when the see was left vacant for a lengthy period and when it was extremely difficult to get a bishop to administer confirmation or to ordain new clergy. The break with Rome finally came in 1713 with the issuing by the Pope of the Bull 'Unigenitus', but the Cathedral Chapter of Utrecht elected Cornelius Steenoven in 1723 who was then consecrated by Bishop Varlet of Babylon who was at the time living in refuge in the Netherlands.

A century and a half later, when the First Vatican Council of 1870 ended abruptly, the German and Swiss theologians (who had been bitterly opposed by the Ultramontane party of Roman Catholics) continued to be attacked because of their objection to Papal Infallibility, and were eventually excommunicated. It was natural that the breakaway Catholic groups of Germany, Austria and Switzerland should, therefore, look to Utrecht for support and leadership, and for episcopal orders in the establishment of their small churches which they claimed were fully Catholic in essence, though non-Papal and free of Vatican control. Other Churches such as the Polish National Catholic Church have since joined the Union of Utrecht.

Since the Second World War, all the churches in Europe have worked more closely together in repairing the ravages caused by the war. Pope John XXIII brought in a new era with the Second Vatican Council, and with his striving for Christian unity. This was seen in 1966 when the Old Catholic and Roman Catholic Bishops in the Netherlands issued a joint Pastoral Letter in November calling for a better understanding between the two Churches. In order to re-open Old Catholic/Roman Catholic discussions, Pope Paul VI agreed to abrogate the two pre-conditions that the Old Catholic Church gave assent to the two Papal Pronouncements, the Formulary of Alexander VII and the Bull 'Unigenitus' of Clement XI.

Today, the need for understanding and unity between the Churches is as great and pressing as ever. With the setting up of Anglican-Orthodox Joint Doctrinal Discussions and with the Anglican-Roman Catholic International Commission as well as plans for Covenanting for Unity with the Free Churches in England, it is to be hoped that the Bonn Agreement of 1931 and the subsequent full communion between Anglicans and Old Catholics will have a positive role and influence and that this book will likewise be of use 'ut omnes unum sint'. To all its contributors, and especially to its editor Dr. Gordon Huelin, I would express my warmest appreciation.

JOHN GIBRALTAR

Acknowledgements

Among those who have contributed to the making of this book I would mention members of the Executive Committee of the Society of St. Willibrord, and in particular the Revd. Alan Cole, now in Bonn, who masterminded it in the early stages and made himself responsible for initial contacts with the various authors. It is with deep regret that I have to record the deaths of two of those members, Jack Witten and Nancy Stamp, both of whom eagerly looked forward to seeing the volume in print. The kindness and generous hospitality extended by Peggy van Vliet and Archbishop and Mrs. Kok during my visit to Holland will long remain a happy memory. Canon Christopher Hill and Mrs. Jane Houston at Lambeth Palace readily put at my disposal the archives of the Archbishop's Counsellors on Foreign Relations. I have in the notes appended to my own chapter referred to others who assisted me personally, but I must express here on behalf of all concerned the debt of gratitude owed to Miss Audrey Bayley of the Oxford University Press for her care in ensuring that this should be a worthy publication. Finally, my wife deserves thanks for having undertaken the laborious but necessary task of preparing an index.

GORDON HUELIN

Contents

List of Plates

(between pp. 84–5)

1

An Assessment of the Bonn Agreement

Robert Runcie

It is a pleasure for me to write this short introduction to the Golden Jubilee Book on the Bonn Agreement. In July 1981 I concelebrated the Eucharist with Archbishop Marinus Kok in Westminster Abbey on the actual date of the Jubilee, and I also joined the Archbishop of Utrecht at the high Altar of his Cathedral for the feast of St. Willibrord the following November.

This book mainly consists of a historical study and pastoral description of the Old Catholic Churches of the Union of Utrecht. But some analysis and evaluation of the Bonn Agreement is also surely called for. In attempting to do this I do not want to claim any very specialist knowledge of the Old Catholic Churches, and this very disclaimer allows me to pay tribute to the Bishop of Chichester, Dr. Eric Kemp, who is certainly a specialist in Old Catholic matters and has done more than anybody else on the Anglican side to further the relationship between the two traditions.

My task in evaluating the Bonn Agreement is made considerably easier by the work done by one who is neither an Anglican nor an Old Catholic: Dr. Lukas Vischer of the Protestant Office for Ecumenism in Switzerland, and formerly Director of the Faith and Order Secretariat of the World Council of Churches. It was a courageous instinct which prompted the Old Catholic bishops to choose to invite Dr. Vischer to deliver a lecture on the Bonn Agreement in the light of the ecumenical movement during the second part of the Jubilee celebrations in Utrecht in November 1981. That they could have made no better choice those who heard the lecture will testify. From his long and wide experience of ecumenical debate Dr. Vischer brought a rich sympathy of understanding to the Bonn Agreement. But this did not affect his precise judgement and careful questions.

On the morning following his lecture I preached in the Old Catholic Cathedral. I said then that he was raising important questions which deserved some answer. I shall take this opportunity of restating the questions and pointing to the direction where I see the answers lying.

In being invited to speak of the Bonn Agreement, Lukas Vischer thought of himself as 'a kind of friend of both the bridegroom and the bride'. He went on to ask if he could also be 'a fool at the feast and raise a few questions'. He thought the Bonn Agreement had had a lack of impact on other unity discussions – and with certain exceptions this is true. But, wisely, he did not go on to dismiss the Bonn Agreement because other traditions have sought different models of unity. He saw the continuing relevance and importance of the Agreement in its ecclesiology. 'The thesis I should like to defend is that the ecclesiology implicit in the agreement is perhaps the soundest basis for real progress in the ecumenical movement.' Coming from one who has had such unique experience of the ecumenical pilgrimage this is high praise indeed. Yet most Anglicans will not be aware that there is an implicit ecclesiology in the Bonn Agreement. A coherent and systematic Anglican approach to ecclesiology is urgently needed, both for Anglican self-definition and for the development of our relations with other Churches. When we look at Anglican appeals for 'intercommunion' with Rome and the Orthodox, or at the way in which decisions have been taken about the ordination of women, we look almost in vain for an Anglican exposition of a theology of the church local and universal.

The Bonn Agreement, on the contrary, contains an implicit ecclesiology which Lukas Vischer sees as highly significant:

The emphasis is on the Church as a eucharistic communion. Jesus Christ is present wherever and whenever the Eucharist is celebrated. The episcopal ministry is to be understood as a service within this eucharistic fellowship. It helps to secure the cohesion of each local church in its life and witness and, at the same time, to make possible the common life and witness of all local churches in a universal conciliar fellowship.

Anglicans and Old Catholics have been led to this understanding of the Church by different historical developments. It was in opposition to the excessive claims of the Roman See that both churches developed their concept of the Church as a communion of local churches.

I hope Anglicans will ponder on this assessment, and even begin to think again about the theology of the church which Lukas Vischer believes is implicit in the Bonn Agreement. But it is not easy to get contemporary Anglicans to realize that any theology of the church is important. It is a cinderella subject amongst us. Yet this was not always so, and earlier Anglicans did not neglect to study the nature of the church. Certainly that 'classical' Anglican Richard Hooker held that the universal church was manifest in the local church in a way which did not make all depend upon a pyramidical structure with the Bishop of Rome as the apex. Nor was he a congregationalist. In a characteristically quaint way he tries to hold together the local and the universal in the image of seas and the ocean:

In which consideration, as the main body of the sea being one, yet within divers precincts hath divers names, so the Catholic Church is in like sort divided into a number of distinct Societies, every one of which is termed a Church within itself.[1]

Because of an apologetic necessity to justify the position of the Church of England against the attacks of both Papists and Puritans, it was essential that sixteenth and seventeenth century Anglicans had a clear ecclesiology. Nor is an Anglican concern for ecclesiology entirely confined to those centuries. John Keble's Assize Sermon was precisely about the nature of the church, and one of the most important features of the Oxford Movement was its affirmation of the Branch Theory, unsatisfactory as it may seem today.[2] Nor has this century been without those Anglicans who have thought and written about the theology of the Church – from Charles Gore to Stephen Neill. But I think Stephen Sykes is right in saying that contemporary Anglicanism fails to take ecclesiology seriously as a theological subject.[3]

Yet here is an international Reformed ecumenist saying that the ecclesiology implicit in the Bonn Agreement is highly significant for all the churches. And we have not recognized it. Lukas Vischer says the Bonn Agreement 'is both an invitation and a criticism within the ecumenical movement: an invitation to the Churches to return to the tradition of the early Church and a criticism of the Churches for having abandoned this tradition either by exaggerating the authority of the hierarchy, especially the authority of the Pope, or by weakening the allegiance to the heritage of the early Church.'

In fact one of the most remarkable developments in ecumenical theology in the last few years has been an almost unnoticed convergence in ecclesiology: the church as a eucharistic communion of local churches. This can be seen not only in Anglican discussion with the

Roman Catholic[4] and Orthodox Churches,[5] but also in the wider horizon of the Faith and Order Commission of the World Council of Churches in which Lukas Vischer as a former Secretary of the Commission has taken a leading part.[6]

His insight is therefore a profound one which has implications for the whole ecumenical movement. Paradoxically, the Bonn Agreement's implicit ecclesiology may well be more important than what was explicitly accepted. Perhaps this implicit agreement on the nature of the church is the reason for the surprising brevity of the Agreement itself, and the extraordinary fact that it only took a day to achieve. In my experience it is certainly true that unconscious differences in the understanding of the church make agreement on other issues impossible.

But if the implicit ecclesiological insight of the Bonn Agreement is profound, the actual impact of the Agreement has been frankly disappointing. Many reasons for this can be offered, not least because the two traditions are geographically and culturally separate from each other, but Vischer suggests that one reason was the nature of the Bonn Agreement itself:

It has to be said that, in certain respects, the agreement does not correspond but rather contradicts the vision of the Church which is the deepest inspiration of the two traditions. This I need to explain. The agreement establishes not communion but intercommunion. There is no communiun when two churches expressly declare that they continue to remain independent entities. The Bonn Agreement is basically no more than a declaration of mutual recognition. It requires no change from the parties but respects the status quo of both communions. In practice, especially in the eyes of other churches, they continue to live and witness as before.

The first sentence of the Bonn Agreement illustrates the difficulty very poignantly. It reads: 'Each communion recognizes the catholicity and independence of the other and maintains its own.' The positive meaning of the sentence is clear: each Church recognizes in the other the gift of catholicity and, while respecting the jurisdictional independence of the other Church, offers *communio in sacris* in all respects. But the phrasing also reveals the hidden contradiction: 'and maintains its own catholicity'. How can churches be catholic if they 'maintain' their 'own' catholicity? Is it not a contradiction in terms to speak of my 'own' catholicity?

Anglicans and Old Catholics are in the debt of Lukas Vischer for pointing out this fallacy. Catholicity is the relation of the local church to the universal church. Even if we wish to 'maintain our own catholicity' we do not have the power to do so except in our relations with *other* churches.

To maintain an isolated independence is, then, to deny catholicity. Anglicans should have recognized this from their own experience within the Anglican Communion. In 1963 the Communion published an important Report entitled *Mutual Responsibility and Interdependence in the Body of Christ*.[7] In the Introduction Archbishop Michael Ramsey also hinted at its ecumenical implications: 'What is at present called the Wider Episcopal Fellowship is not an organization but an exploring of the implications of full communion in the Church of God.' But the exploration never took place – it was even discouraged. The implications of communion with the United Churches of India, Pakistan and Bangladesh have been explored almost as little as that with the Old Catholics, or that with the churches of Sweden and Finland.

On the Old Catholic side there has been an intuition that communion implies more than mutual recognition. Decisions on matters of church order inevitably affect relationships between churches because the ordained ministry is the main link between one church community and another. It was not that the Old Catholic Churches claimed that they had any right to veto an Anglican decision on the ordination of women. Indeed the Bonn Agreement seems, on the face of it, to allow such a decision.[8] But they did feel it was a matter to be decided with more appreciation for wider Christian counsel.

Quite distinct from this particular issue was the Old Catholic request for membership of the Anglican Consultative Council.[9] But this proved unacceptable and Archbishop Ramsey's promptings towards the exploration of the meaning of 'full communion' – which the Bonn Agreement is now said to achieve rather than intercommunion – were not followed through. Not, at least, until the last meeting of the Council which said the following:

The question we ask ... is whether being in communion has any implications beyond the simple possibility of sacramental sharing and exchange of ministers. This is not primarily a question of exact terminology but rather a question about the need of the churches for a richer fellowship. Communion must be understood as involving more than *liturgical* celebration: it surely implies a visible sharing together in the common *life* of the Body of Christ.[10]

It will be clear that I hope the Anglican Communion will pursue this question and look again at its official relations with the Old Catholic Churches – and not only them but all the episcopal churches with which we have a relation of communion. I am not suggesting a multiplicity of international meetings for 'jet set' pre-lates. Institutions and structures should be sufficient for mutual need and no more. In fact the Anglican Consultative Council spoke of 'some regional form of fellowship which would bring appropriate churches together in common counsel and exchange'. I hope this will be explored not for the sake of meetings or institutions but to give reality to our 'communion' and so enable what Lukas Vischer spoke of as 'joint confession'.

The word 'confession' is not an easy one in English but I take him to mean a 'joint witness and a common pastoral application of the Gospel'. But this requires common counsel and pastoral exchange if a renewed vision is to emerge which will liberate pastoral energies. At the time of the Bonn Agreement there was hope on both sides that horizons would be widened in this way. The Old Catholics believed the Agreement would help them overcome their minority situation.[11] Anglicans saw a new universality being provided by their relation with Continental Christians.[12] Surely this is precisely the commu-nion of 'life' which is still needed but requires an appropriate instru-mentality for its achievement. The Anglican Communion can give to Old Catholics the vision of a world-wide Church and the pastoral variety and openness which comes with a tradition which, though originating in a particular culture, now flourishes in others widely different from the Anglo-Saxon. The Old Catholics can, even in their comparatively small number, give Anglicans access to a European Christian culture which they have not formerly experienced. This is especially true for the Diocese in Europe and the Convocation of American Churches in Europe. Theologically, too, there is a wide area for mutual enrichment. We have a common past tradition of 'criticism', particularly the criticism of Papal authority. Yet in other ways we have trodden very different paths. Perhaps Old Catholics can learn something from an Anglican pragmatic pastoral approach to contemporary issues facing the churches. I believe Anglicans can certainly learn much from the fidelity of the Old Catholics to the patristic tradition and their appeal to the Vincentian Canon in disputed questions as a test of catholicity: *quod ubique, quod semper, quod ab omnibus creditum est.* It must not be thought that this necessarily leads to inflexibility. The Old Catholic Churches have long since been using the Nicene Creed in its original form while I still urge the Church of England to do so – less the *Filioque* clause!

Though minority churches, the mere existence of the Old Catholic Churches has a theological importance: a non-Roman Catholic Western tradition which does not have the roots of its divergence from Rome in the Reformation. It is not surprising that the Orthodox Churches have looked with favour on the Old Catholics, and this is in itself important.

I cannot complete an assessment of the Bonn Agreement without speaking of our common dialogue with Rome. The Old Catholics have an agreement with the Roman Catholic Church which is being implemented by stages. It amounts to partial communion.[13] Anglicans are less advanced but 1982 has seen the Final Report of the Anglican/Roman Catholic International Commission, and also the visit of Pope John Paul II to Canterbury Cathedral with a hoped-for step forward in relations. With the Orthodox, Anglicans and Old Catholics can recognize the Bishop of Rome as *primus inter pares*, a primacy of responsibility: a service of unity for all the churches. But we do not recognize the jurisdictional supremacy as defined at the First Vatican Council. Here we stand on common ground and welcome the way in which the Roman Catholic Church is seeking to find new ways of expressing the Roman primacy. To Anglicans and Old Catholics, as well as Orthodox, a renewal in the manner of the exercise of the Roman primacy is also of vital importance.

Having said this, there is a historical aptness in an Old Catholic-Roman Catholic reconciliation which I do not believe the Bonn Agreement should stand in the way of. Indeed, if reconciliation is possible with the Old Catholics – rejecting as they do the supremacy of the Pope as defined at the First Vatican Council of 1870 – then a way may be opened for others, Orthodox, Anglican and Protestant. If, however, an acceptance of the First Vatican Council is the *sine qua non* for the healing of a schism, which has not otherwise involved the radical divergence of the two traditions, it is not likely that the healing of the Anglican-Roman Catholic breach will be offered at a cheaper price. Anglicans should therefore give every encouragement to the restoration of Old Catholic-Roman Catholic unity, both for its own sake and for wider ecumenical gain. If a way round the Roman centralist ideology of the nineteenth century is discovered, the witness of the See of Utrecht to an earlier view of the church will not have been in vain: the same view of the church which Anglicans rediscovered in their own debate with Rome and the underlying basis of the Bonn Agreement.

To draw the threads of this short assessment together, I repeat my endorsement of Lukas Vischer's thesis that the importance of the Bonn Agreement lies not so much in its content as its underlying presupposition: the church as a eucharistic communion of local churches. Yet the profound implications of this insight have not been recognized or acted upon – the text of the Agreement almost militates against them with its un-Catholic stress on *'independence'*. But there are hopeful signs amongst Anglicans and Old Catholics that the deep significance of 'being in communion' are at last being recognized. 'Being in communion' means an intimate sharing in both faith and witness: the ecumenical life of the church must express this.

When the Bonn Agreement was accepted by the Convocation of Canterbury there was debate as to what had actually been achieved. There was some recognition that the relationship was less than the visible unity which is the ecumenical goal. Others argued that 'intercommunion' was the only proper goal to seek.[14] Perhaps the Bonn Agreement can teach us the dangers of seeking only a comfortable half-way house on the ecumenical pilgrimage. Unity by stages is one thing: acquiescence – even contentment – with less than the full mutual participation unity implies is another. If Anglicans doubt this in relation to the Old Catholic Churches, let them consider the serious diminishment of our catholicity we have suffered by accepting certain aspects of the Bonn Agreement in our relationships with the United Churches of North and South India, Pakistan and Bangladesh. While these churches are 'in communion' they are not part of 'the Communion'. We have the paradoxical achievement of sacramental communion without that which it is intended to signify: ecclesial communion. Yet the Bonn Agreement presupposes a communion of churches.

I hope the Jubilee of the Bonn Agreement and beyond can be an opportunity for Anglicans to think more seriously about the models of unity behind the various ecumenical dialogues with a view to the sure advancement of a unity in a communion of churches. In one sense the Bonn Agreement was an engagement rather than a marriage. Let the coming years see a closer relationship with the Old Catholic Churches and the other episcopal churches with whom we are in communion. This is surely what our mutual communion as churches demands. Let engagement become marriage.

NOTES

1. Richard Hooker, *The Laws of Ecclesiastical Polity*, Book III, ch. 1, 14.
2. While not the first to think of the church in this way – Roman, Orthodox and Anglican – William Palmer is usually acknowledged to have been the first to expound the theory with precision in his *Treatise on the Church of Christ*, 1838.
3. S. Sykes, *The Integrity of Anglicanism* (1978), ch. 6.
4. See the Introduction and 'Authority in the Church I', para. 8 of *The Final Report* of the Anglican-Roman Catholic International Commission (1982).
5. See 'The Church as the Eucharistic Community', *Anglican-Orthodox Dialogue: The Moscow Agreed Statement* (esp. paras. 22–4), Anglican-Orthodox Joint Doctrinal Commission (1977).
6. See 'One Eucharist', para. 27 *One Baptism One Eucharist and a Mutually Recognized Ministry* (1975). Lukas Vischer puts it this way in his Utrecht lecture: 'The new common ecumenical emphasis on the local church understood as a eucharistic community has its source in the rediscovery of the early Church. The description of the "unity we seek" as "conciliar fellowship" was developed on the basis of an intensive study of the conciliar process in the early centuries. Without the "ressourcement patristique", I believe, the Faith and Order texts on baptism, eucharist and ministry would not have been possible.'
7. Ed. by Stephen F. Bayne, Jr.
8. Bishop Eric Kemp argues otherwise elsewhere in this volume.
9. See the Report of the Second Meeting of the Anglican Consultative Council (pp. 65–6) and the Report of the Third Meeting (p. 68), 1973 and 1976.
10. Report of the Fifth Meeting of the Anglican Consultative Council: Unity and Ecumenical Affairs, para. 8, 1981.
11. *Internationale Kirchliche Zeitschrift*, 21, 1931, 3.
12. *Chronicle of the Convocation of Canterbury*, 1932.
13. Based on the Old Catholic *Züricher Nota* of 1969. See the essay by Dr. Gordon Huelin in this volume: 'Old Catholics and Ecumenism'.
14. *Chronicle of the Convocation of Canterbury*, 1932.

2

Constitutions of the Old Catholic Churches

MARINUS KOK

The Old Catholic churches united in the Union of Utrecht are very dissimilar in origin and history. It is because of this that the organization of these churches is very different. However, the national churches share one characteristic: they are all founded on the constitutions of the Early Church as these are laid down in the Ecumenical Councils.

In the Early Church the bishop was elected by the clergy and the laity together, or by a representative group of the latter. The whole accent was on the rights of the local church to elect its own bishop and to seek permission and approval for his consecration from the neighbouring bishops. Through the centuries this pattern underwent considerable change. In the Western Church legal thinking became so influential, and the institutional character of the church received so much emphasis, that on the whole the church was identified with the church which found its focus and unity in Rome. In this way a church, caught in a continually extending system of legal regulations, was identified with the communion of faith as intended by the Lord (John ch. 17 v. 21). In this way the ideal of the Ecclesia Primitiva, the ideal of a communion of faith in collegial solidarity adhering to that which always, everywhere and by all has been believed, is left.

Right from the beginning protests have been voiced against this view. St. Cyprian may acknowledge the primacy of St. Peter and the cathedra in Rome, but he also maintains the cooperation of the one episcopacy, because the apostles have all received equal authority from the Lord. It is in the primacy of St. Peter that the episcopacy finds its unity.[1]

The Orthodox churches in the East have always thought more in terms such as communion of the faithful, of the local churches and of their bishops. In that respect they remained faithful to the sober New Testament principles, more so than the Western Church which gradually accepted a structure of a one type monarchical-absolutist-centralized church.[2]

Pope Leo the Great (440–461) strongly stimulated this development, referring to the texts concerning St. Peter (Matthew ch. 16: vv. 18–20, Luke ch. 22: vv. 31–2 and John ch. 21: v. 15). In many ways the papacy proved to be a blessing and a stronghold for many in the perilous centuries after the migration. The presumption of power by the popes during the Middle Ages steadily increased, and reached its culmination under Innocent III (1198–1216), and Boniface VIII (1294–1303) who formulated in extremely bold words the papal claims to world rule in the bull 'Unam Sanctam'.

The Councils of Constance and Basle (1414–18 and 1431–49) tried in vain to defend the conciliar principle of the Early Church against the increasing curialism of Rome. The only result was that the national states more and more kept the national churches in tutelage, the papacy remaining deaf to the call for reform at all levels in the church. The stream of episcopalism and conciliarism later found its way in Gallicanism, Febronianism, Jansenism and Josephinism. But here political aims often proved stronger than ecclesiological principles. The national states through these movements tried to increase their influence on the church.

It is not within the scope of this short article to define in detail the episcopalian and conciliar movements in the course of history, but rather to indicate the outline. The continual conflict between episcopalism and papalism nowhere resulted in a schism; but in the Netherlands the ancient Church of Utrecht insisted on the rights and privileges of the local church, which did not have to conform automatically to the infallible point of view of the Roman pontiff, especially regarding the much disputed matter of Jansenism.

The Church of Utrecht

Of old there was in the Church of Utrecht a tendency as a local church to follow its own views and traditions in matters of faith. On this point the church certainly remained faithful to its founder St. Willibrord, and to the spirituality of the Irish-Scottish church that as a local church left such a strong mark on Anglo-Saxon Christianity. In the Middle Ages the 'Brothers of the Common Life', the so-called modern devotion, developed a very special spirituality which had its influence far beyond the Dutch borders, remaining critical towards the accepted piety of the Catholic Church of that period. The Brothers of the Common Life, of whom must be mentioned especially Gerard Groote and Thomas à Kempis, occupied themselves with Scripture, the Fathers, meditation and teaching.

During the period of the Reformation the Catholic Church of the Netherlands went through a very difficult phase, church properties were confiscated by the ruling Calvinists, and the clergy were persecuted. Everything the Inquisition of the Spanish king Philip II and the 'Iron Duke' Alva did to the Protestants, was revenged by the Calvinists on the Catholics. But even in these grim times the greater part of the people remained faithful to the old church and the old faith and thus the Catholic church managed to continue to function as a hidden church, though not without great sacrifices. A sense of freedom and tolerance, characteristic features of the Dutch nature, soon helped to alleviate the contrasts and make life bearable again for the Catholics in the Netherlands.

The difficulties that followed in the seventeenth century came rather from inside than from outside the church. During the days of the Counter-Reformation many regular priests, especially Jesuits, came to Holland with the intention of restoring the old church to its former glory. Their way of thinking and their methods in no way agreed with the spirituality of the Dutch priests who had lived through the trials of persecution and confessed to a simple, chastened Catholicism. Indulgences, pilgrimages, rosaries and the adoration of the Holy Virgin were in Holland far less important than the reading of Scripture and meditation. Differences in training and in sociological background widened the gap between the two groups. Soon conflicts arose, resulting in a wide range of complaints from the side of the regular clergy in Rome. These complaints doubled in number when part of the clergy was accused of 'Jansenism'. The majority of the Dutch clergy were educated in Louvain, the nursery of Augustinianism. At the University of Louvain Cornelius Jansen from Acquoi in the Netherlands, taught theology for a great many years. He then studied the works of St. Augustine and became familiar with the polemics in his writings, but he was also very impressed by the greatness of thought of this Father of the Church. Later Jansen became Bishop of Ypres, but until his death in 1638 he remained fascinated by the works of St. Augustine, especially those dealing with grace in God's plan of salvation. In Holland there was of course great interest in the posthumous work of Bishop Jansen called *The Augustinus; or the Doctrine of St. Augustine on the Health, Sickness and Medicine of the Soul*. In this work, a series of quotations from this Father of the Church, the author proved how only the grace of God is able to rescue the fallen nature of man. In this book Jansen strongly condemned the teachings of the Jesuit Molina, who, in the steps of St. Augustine's opponent Pelagius, taught the faithful that man when trying hard will not be left without the grace of God.

The book of Jansen was accused by the Jesuits in Rome and ultimately condemned in 1665 by pope Alexander VII in the notorious 'Formulary of Alexander VII'. This formulary had to be signed by bishops, priests and all those taking religious vows at their consecration. It is easily understood that the book of Jansenius with its Augustinian theory of grace based on the gospel, met with great response in a country marked by the 'sola gratia' of Calvinism. Moreover, a great many priests, who besides having studied in Louvain were also trained by the Oratorians in Paris, felt related in the spirit with the spirituality of the French convent Port-Royal. Here a severe and deeply religious piety was practised, being the spiritual fruit of the thinking of St. Augustine as recorded by Jansen, and which his friend and fellow-combatant Jean du Vergier de Hauranne, afterwards abbot of St. Cyran, maintained as confessor of the abbey of Port-Royal.

However, this does not mean that by then in the church of Utrecht, any deviating religious opinion was adhered to, but that some refused to sign a formulary which condemned propositions supposedly from the book of Jansen that were nowhere to be found in that book. The refusal by many to sign the formulary ultimately resulted in the deposition by Rome of Peter Codde the then Archbishop of Utrecht, because he too, before his consecration, had refused to sign the formulary. During the following years when the Metropolitan Chapter of Utrecht refused to accept Rome's decision on Codde, the conflict was sharpened by the question whether the Catholic Church in Holland during the storms of the Reformation had not been changed into a mission-church, or whether the Apostolic Vicars during the days of oppression had continued as independent ordinarii of the see of Utrecht, and whether the decimated Chapter of Utrecht was still the legal successor to the medieval Chapters. With no understanding for the extremely difficult circumstances in which the Church of Utrecht stood its ground as a local church, Rome abandoned this church because it allowed no deviation from the line as set out by Rome.

Important ecclesiastical lawyers like Bernard van Espen (d. 1728) and Joan. Christiaan van Erkel (d. 1734) could, drawing from ancient sources, write extensive treatises in defence of the Church of Utrecht, but Rome remained relentless and excommunicated the successors of Archbishop Codde who were elected by the Chapter to the see of Utrecht. In a recently published study of Roman Catholic origin it is again explicitly stated that Rome in this case showed little understanding of developments in a local church, a church in a diaspora situation.[3] Yet in the years which followed, the Church of Utrecht tried hard to keep in its preaching, practice and church organization to the tradition of the Latin Church in order not to be accused of heresy.

This was clearly expressed by the Provincial Council of 1763 which wholly conformed with post-Tridentine Catholicism. Longing to make peace with Rome, however, the Council went too far. Looking back on the developments in the Latin Church until the First Vatican Council, the next generation found it necessary to reconsider the decrees of the Council of Utrecht on the papacy and the schismatic nature of the Eastern churches.[4] Through contacts with protest-movements, arising in the Catholic churches in Germany and Switzerland after the proclamation of the dogma on Papal Infallibility in 1870 during Vatican I, new prospects arose in the desperate situation of the little church of Utrecht. Hesitating at first when confronted with the rather radical views from abroad, including a certain amount of modernism of which the Dutch Old Catholics were rightly apprehensive, the twentieth century brought the breakthrough of a renovating movement. This attempted to offer and proclaim a purified and original Catholicism. Even though the Dutch bishops refused to take part in the consecration of the first Swiss bishop, Eduard Herzog, in 1876 in Rheinfelden because of the radical tendencies in the Swiss Church, and even though they raised objections against the radical denial of the papacy at the consultations about a closer relationship between the Old Catholic Churches as effected in 1889, this renovating movement also had its influence in the Netherlands.

This became visible in the liturgical renewal when in 1909 Latin was replaced by Dutch in the liturgy as well as in the church ordinances. Compulsory celibacy for priests was abolished in 1922 as it was in the Old Catholic churches abroad. In 1919 a National Synod and a Synodal Council were instituted, followed in 1922 by Regulations for Parochial Councils. These new institutions and regulations did not function properly right from the start; structure and wording needed revision repeatedly, but all the same a choice was made with regard to the course to be taken. In the controversy with Rome the Fathers ardently defended the conciliar philosophy, and this was now extended from the top to the base in order to give to all members participation and co-responsibility in the same way as it functioned in the Early Church concerning the position of the church in the world. This coincided with the awakening of the faithful to their rights and duties in the church, and with their demand to participate in its affairs.

This development continued after the Second World War. Until the beginning of the present century in all matters concerning ecclesiastical law the answer was looked for in the Corpus Iuris Canonici and the explanation of this in the work of Bernard van Espen *Ius Ecclesiasticum Universum*.

After 1920 a start was made in composing a Constitution for the Old Catholic Church of the Netherlands. This was finished in 1950 and it came into force on 24 April of that year. A new edition with alterations and additions was published in 1972 and came into force on 7 November of the same year, this being the feast of St. Willibrord. According to the ancient clauses of the Corpus Iuris the bishops still retained all power in spiritual and temporal matters in the church. When composing the new Constitution, especially in the revised edition a new course was taken. The accent was no longer solely on the episcopal nature of the church, but also on its synodal nature.

In the first section of the revised Constitution the rights and duties of the laity are written down: the reading of and the meditation on Holy Scripture, the receiving of the sacraments, the attending of church services, the taking up of tasks to which a person can be called by the church, contributing financially to the church and taking part in the life of the church in its widest sense. Next, attention is paid to the structure in which the laity lives: the parish. The members of the parish offer to the bishop a list of recommendations for the appointment of the members of the parish committee and the churchwardens. The parochial committee has to render account for its management of the parish annually to the bishop. The president of the committee is the priest in charge of the parish or a member of the laity. The parish priest is appointed by the bishop in consultation with the parochial committee.

The next chapter of the revised Constitution deals with the clergy, their training, the task of the priests and their duties and rights. After this a description is given of the tasks and rights of the Metropolitan Chapter of Utrecht and of the clergy of the Haarlem diocese. When the see is vacant, the clergy of the archbishopric of Utrecht, together with a number of lay persons who have been chosen for this duty by the Synod, elect the new archbishop. The same applies to the diocese of Haarlem. The number of lay persons on the electoral roll equals half the number of clergy. The Bishop of Deventer, a titular bishop, is appointed by the archbishop under the so-called 'ius devolutionis'. All the clergy of the church together with a number of lay persons which again equals half the number of clergy, compose a nomination list for the archbishop.[5]

After this follows a chapter of the Provincial Synod of the clergy that is to meet at least once every two years. Usually, however, it meets once a year. Section 7 of the Constitution deals with the bishops, their rights and duties and the relation in which they have to work together: the episcopate. It is made clear that all bishops have equal power and full authority to rule that part of the church which is entrusted to them together with their clergy. The Archbishop of Utrecht is the metropolitan of the Dutch bishops and as such *primus inter pares*. He confirms the election of the Bishop of Haarlem but apart from that he has no power in any other diocese, except when neglect of temporal or spiritual interests is apparent.

The next chapter of the Constitution deals with the Synod. The Synod has an advisory task, especially with regard to the temporal matters in the church. A Synodal Council, elected by the Synod, prepares the meetings of the Synod and executes its decisions. The Synod consists of the clergy in active service, the members of parochial committees, the members of the General Treasury and the Synodal Councillors. It meets annually. Chapter IX of the Constitution deals with the finances of the church and its financial management. The General Treasury is the controlling and advisory organ of the bishops, and is in charge of the financial management and responsible for this to the episcopate after having heard the Synod.

In the last section of the Constitution the legal life of the church is dealt with and an advisory committee of legal ecclesiastical matters is mentioned. This advises the bishops when legal ecclesiastical rules are trespassed, or in the event of uncertainty about the explanation of these rules.

The Synod of 1981 accepted a proposal to arrive at a definite form of episcopal-synodal administration in such a sense that a collegiate administration is instituted. Members of this body are the bishops, with a representation of the clergy and of the laity, and together they administrate and lead the church, each on the strength of his own assignment and responsibility. The bishops in the ministry of their office and according to their personal responsibility in this, keep their right to take independent decisions after hearing the Synod and the Collegiate Administrative Body on spiritual and moral issues. At the moment the Synod continues as an advisory body. In the near future the Committee on Ecclesiastical Law will further develop this new draft.

In this way the Church of Utrecht, though small in numbers, is fully aware of its commission as an independent Catholic Church in Latin Christendom not only to preserve the heritage of the Fathers, but also to carry it out into the world in a manner fitting this period and with all strength available. Only then will the church fulfil its essential task as a local church.

The Old Catholic Churches outside the Netherlands

In the above, the Old Catholic Church of the Netherlands was explicitly described. Officially the church is registered as 'the Roman Catholic Church of the Old Episcopal Clergy'. In the first Article of the Constitution of the Old Catholic Church of the Netherlands it is explicitly stated that this church is: 'the community of Catholic believers residing in the State of the Netherlands under the guidance of the old episcopal clergy and in possession of the apostolic succession through its continuing line of bishops arising from its founder, St. Willibrord'.

Acceptance of this fact implies that the Old Catholic Church of the Netherlands is not the outcome of seccession. As a Catholic church it stems from the origin of Christendom in the Low Countries. The Roman Catholic Church has caused the breach, and by the institution of 'new dioceses' in 1853 it has erected opposing altars, resulting in the situation of two archiepiscopates of Utrecht and two bishops of Haarlem.[6]

The development of Old Catholic Churches in other countries has been totally different. These could be described as 'emergency bodies' of Catholic faithful, who could not reconcile it with their conscience to agree with the developments in the Roman Catholic Church after 1870. As formulated by the famous church historian Ignaz von Döllinger when addressing Archbishop Scherr of Munich: 'As a Christian, as a theologian, as a historian and as a citizen I cannot accept this new dogma.'

Episodes in the Old Catholic movement

In the nineteenth century the episcopalian and the conciliar tendency also found its course in the churches of Germany and Switzerland, but this movement for reformation did not cause a breach in the Catholic church. Again and again the theologians state that from studying the Early Church they find it is the course of the development of the Latin Church into a new judicial-absolutist legal system, and the resulting new conception of the church of Rome as formulated in 1870 which they can no longer support. It is wrong to describe these theologians as the forerunners of the Old Catholic movement, but they all tend towards the structure and the religious experience of the Early Church as is rejected by the official church of Rome. An example of this is seen in somebody like Ignaz Heinrich von Wessenberg, administrator of the diocese of Constance, who in reforming his diocese attracted a lot of attention from the churches of Germany and Switzerland but was condemned by Rome. Also could be mentioned J. M. Sailer (d. 1832), bishop of Regensburg, who as a mystic laid great weight on the inner life of the faithful and from that vision wrote a number of devotional works and prayer-books. Others are the doctors of divinity George Hermes (d. 1831) from Bonn, and Anton Günther (d. 1863) from Vienna.

The historical schools of Tübingen and Munich, to which Ignaz von Döllinger belonged, especially stimulated and laid the foundations for the Old Catholic movement. This is not the right place to explain the historical development of the Old Catholic movement as it took place before and after the First Vatican Council. It should only be stated that the Old Catholic movement from the beginning was guided by three principles:

1.   to protest against the judicial-centralized striving of Vatican I and in the face of this to hold on to the witness of Scripture and the tradition of the undivided church of the first ten centuries;

2.   to build up a church in accordance with the religious views and church ordinances of the Early, undivided Church;

3.   to seek reunion with the divided Christian churches on the basis of the spiritual life of the Early Church.

Of these principles witness was already given at the first Old Catholic Congress, held in Munich in 1871, which was attended by representatives of the Old Catholic movements in Germany, Switzerland and Austria, and also by guests from the Church of Utrecht, the Anglican Church, the Russian Orthodox Church and the Evangelical Church. In this connection should also be mentioned the immense importance in an ecumenical sense of the so-called 'Bonner Unions-Konferenzen' of 1874 and 1875 under the competent leadership of Döllinger, which according to the three above mentioned principles laid the basis for the later negotiations of the Old Catholics with the Anglicans and the Orthodox.

The first bishop of the German Old Catholic Church, Josef Hubert Reinkens was consecrated in 1873 in Rotterdam by the Bishop of Deventer, Hermann Heykamp. In his turn Bishop Reinkens consecrated the first Christ-Catholic bishop for Switzerland, Eduard Herzog in Rheinfelden in 1876. In particular, Professor Walter Munzinger (d. 1873), influenced by the Congress in Munich in 1871, initiated the formation of Christ-Catholic parishes in Switzerland.

The Old Catholic Congress of Constance in September 1873 proved to be of special importance for the Old Catholic Churches which were being formed in Germany and Switzerland. There the draft was accepted for an Old Catholic synodal and parochial ordinance, as drawn up by Professor Johann Friedrich von Schulte (1827–1914). This church ordinance has become the basis for the constitutions of the German, the Swiss, the Austrian and the Czechslovak churches. Here an attempt was made to draft, on the basis of the Early Church ordinance, an episcopal-synodal constitution for the church today. In the general definitions it is explicitly stated that this ordinance is of a provisionary nature. According to this constitution the bishops have the general rights and duties as have always been due to a bishop in the church. The bishop is elected by the Synod. Representatives of clergy and laity from the Synod form together the Synodal Council and assist the bishop in leading the church. The bishop is chairman of the Synod. The Synod is formed by the clergy and the laity. The laity are elected by the parishes. The priest in charge of the parish is elected by the congregation and confirmed and installed by the bishop.

In Switzerland the bishop is a member of the Synodal Council, but he is not its chairman as he is in Germany. The chairman of the Synodal Council and of the Synod are in Switzerland elected by the Synod.[7] A further difference between the German and the Swiss church constitution is that in Germany it is rather built from the top to the base, while in Switzerland it is more from the base to the top. In the Swiss constitution this is clear from the emphasis on the congregations which together compose the church. Of course in Germany as well as in Switzerland political and ideological factors have influenced the realization of the Old Catholic churches (*Kulturkampf*).

In Austria and Czechoslovakia, the latter being formed after the falling apart of the Danube monarchy, the Old Catholic churches experienced strong opposition from the side of the State. Dioceses were founded in Vienna and later for Czechoslovakia in Warnsdorf. The church ordinance of Austria has been completely renewed in 1980 adhering closely to the draft of von Schulte. The bishop in guiding the church is assisted by a Synodal Council. The bishop attends the sessions of the Synodal Council, but is not a member of this body. A lay person is chairman of the Synodal Council and leads the discussions in the Synod. The Synod consists of the members of the Synodal Council, the clergy and representatives of the laity. The bishop is a member and chairman of the Synod. The congregation elects its parish priest, who is then appointed by the bishop with the approval of the Synodal Council. In the new church ordinance the bishop is less dependent on the 'Kirchliche Oberbehörde' than before.

The church of Yugoslavia dates from the 1920s and suffered much from the hands of the Roman Catholic Church before and after the Second World War. As this applies to all other churches in the communist countries this church will also have to try and live with the limiting measures from the side of the State.

The Polish National Catholic Church of America, Canada and Poland has made its own history. It was first and foremost bishop Francis Hodur who in America built up this church with mainly Polish emigrants. Conflicts about the management of the financial resources of the church were in the first instance the reason for breaking with Rome, but an important part was also played by the lack of interest of the Irish and German representatives of the American hierarchy for the needs of the Polish emigrants. Here too the rights of the local church were denied by Rome.

The church in America is governed by the bishop and the General Synod. The Prime Bishop has a lot of power in the ruling of the church together with the other bishops. The Supreme Council is the executive body of the church in which, together with the bishops and representatives of the clergy, lay persons take their place. The General Synod consists of the bishops, the clergy, representatives of the congregations and a number of church organizations. The Synod elects the bishops. The parish priests are appointed by the bishop with the approval of the Parish Committee. The Parish Committee is elected by the members of the congregation with the approval of the bishop.

The centre of the church is in Scranton. After the First World War the Poles from America founded a daughter church in Poland. This church is independent under the name of the 'Polish Catholic Church'. The Prime Bishop has his see in Warsaw. This church suffered great losses during the Second World War, but in the period since the war it has flourished anew.

The Union of Utrecht of 1889

The bishops of the Netherlands, Germany and Switzerland signed a treaty in 1889 that has become known as 'The Declaration of Utrecht'.[8] In this it becomes clear that the bishops keep to the belief of the Church of the first ten centuries as it is expressed by the Ecumenical Councils.

Thus the dogmas of 1854 and 1870 declaring the Immaculate Conception of Mary and the Papal Infallibility are rejected, while the position of the bishop of Rome as *primus inter pares* is accepted. Rejected also are the Bulls 'Unigenitus' (1713) directed against the book *Réflexions morales* by Paschasius Quesnel, and 'Auctorem Fidei' (containing the condemnation of the Synod of Pistoia of 1786), and the Syllabus Errorum of 1864. The Council of Trent is rejected in as far as concerns the decrees on discipline in the church. The doctrinal rulings are only accepted in as far as they are in agreement with the doctrine of the Early Church.

There follows a paragraph on the eucharist and finally a paragraph in which the hope is expressed for unity in the churches based on the belief of the undivided church. This document is the foundation of the communion of the Old Catholic churches, and has to be signed by every bishop on entering the Union of Utrecht.

The declaration of 1889 is nearly a hundred years old and it certainly is not an infallible document for now and eternity. There are many reasons for adapting the rulings of the bishops in 1889 to the present situation in which the churches live and have relationships with one another in a world-wide ecumenical fellowship. Rulings on papal bulls from a distant past do not mean very much to Christians today, even when behind these rulings important truths are hidden.

The foundation on which the Old Catholic Churches are built remains important, namely the word from St. Vincent of Lérins in his *Commonitorium* of the year 434: 'Id teneamus, quod ubique, quod semper, quod ab omnibus creditum est; hoc est etenim vere propieque catholicum' ('we maintain what everywhere and always by everyone has been believed, this being truly and actually catholic'). To this immediately may be added another word from the Early Church, which is always used as a guide in negotiations with other churches : 'In necessariis unitas; in dubiis libertas; in omnibus caritas'. ('In the essential unity; in the doubtful liberty; in everything charity.')

On these principles the Bonn Agreement of 2 July 1931 was also founded. This is the agreement between Anglicans and Old Catholics. Of great importance for the future relationship between Anglicans, Old Catholics and other churches is to consider together what are 'all the essentials of the Christian faith' to which each church has committed itself to remain faithful (Bonn Agreement, 3).

With regard to the contacts with the Roman Catholic Church it is important to clarify what is meant by the 'historical primacy of the bishop of Rome' as it is formulated in the Bishops' Declaration of 1889. Here a start was made by the declaration of the Old Catholic International Bishops' Conference of 1970 in which it is stated that the Petrine office has the task to strengthen the whole church in truth and love and to maintain the bond between all bishops and churches.

It will be the task of the Anglican, Old Catholic and Orthodox theologians in conference with Roman Catholic theologians to create clarity on this point, especially on the point of the manner in which the ministering Petrine office can find its place in the episcopal-synodal church structure.

The International Bishops' Conference

On the same day as the Utrecht Episcopal Declaration was issued, an agreement was drawn up about the mutual official relation between the bishops and regulations for the International Bishops' Conference of the Union of Utrecht. The last time these two documents were revised was in 1974. In this it is stated that the churches represented by the bishops of the Union of Utrecht are in full communion with one another on the strength of the Declaration of 1889. It is also stipulated that the International Bishops' Conference has authority to adopt a position in controversial questions on faith and order. The bishops cannot come to agreements with other churches unless these are first discussed with, and authorized by, all bishops.

It is also stated that the International Bishops' Conference possesses no jurisdiction in the separate churches of the Utrecht Union, but is responsible for safeguarding the communion of the Old Catholic churches and their bishops. In the regulations is stipulated that the Archbishop of Utrecht, as occupying the most ancient see in the Union of Utrecht, is chairman of the International Bishops' Conference. As such he is *primus inter pares* among the bishops, and this position is comparable to the one the Archbishop of Canterbury occupies in the Anglican Communion. The International Bishops' Conference meets at least once a year and more often as is necessary.

As the Union of Utrecht and the International Bishops' Conference connected with it are now nearly a hundred years old, it is desirable to reflect anew on the essence of the Utrecht Union. Is it right to compare it with the synods of the Early Church, and has it therefore the same rights and authority? Or is it rather an 'emergency bandage'?. If it is the latter, should great caution be taken with regard to new statements on faith and order, and it is advisable that the Conference should limit itself to the safeguarding and passing on of the received treasure of faith and order, translating this into the language of today? Or is its task to define the position of the Utrecht Union amidst the other churches in the ecumenical community and its relation to other 'emergency bandages' such as the Lambeth Conference and the councils or synods of churches in East and West? As is stipulated in the declaration of the International Bishops'

Conference of 1970, the pre-eminence should be given to promoting 'the development of a conciliary communion of all churches in which the original serving character of a Petrine primacy finds a new fulfilment'.

Rightly, the bishops ask all persons responsible for the guidance of the churches to 'become more conscious of their joint responsibility to create room for a new, truly General Council that can speak and decide for all Christians.' In this manner the International Bishops' Conference of the Union of Utrecht can work for the next twenty or thirty years, fulfilling a truly historical commission, and giving essential service towards the fulfilment of the ideal of the churches becoming one and working together in serving the well-being of the world today.

NOTES

1. St. Cyprian, *De Catholicae Ecclesiae Unitate*, ch. 4.
2. Hans Küng, *Die Kirche*, p. 509 (cf. p. 446 in the English translation *The Church* (1967) [editor]).
3. J. Y. H. A. Jacobs, *Joan. Christiaan van Erkel (1654–1734): Advocate for a local church.*
4. Declaration of the Old Catholic bishops of the Netherlands 7 June 1922.
5. In this paragraph by 'clergy' is meant the priests and deacons of the church.
6. Bull *Ex qua die* by Pope Pius IX.
7. Especially important in this connection is the Pastoral Letter of the Swiss bishop Urs Küry (d. 1976): *Unsere Synode* (cf. Urs Küry, *Hirtenbriefe*, Allschwil, 1978, p. 187), in which the ideal picture of a church synod is described.
8. cf. 'The Declaration of Utrecht', included in the *Report of the Lambeth Conference of 1930*, p. 142, as well as in C. B. Moss, *The Old Catholic Movement* (2nd ed.) p. 281.

3

Old Catholicism Since World War II

Peter Amiet

When Urs Küry,[1] in his last pastoral letter to Swiss Old Catholics in 1972, called the post-war period, 'the moment for theological reappraisal and ecumenical progress', he pin-pointed the issue convincingly. A new phase was obviously beginning in Old Catholic history, imprinted with the consequences of war, devastation and reconstruction.

Briefly, let us survey individual national churches, beginning with the Dutch Old Catholic Church. During the war, it had distinguished itself by an impressive even valiant, exercise in neighbourly love. Consequent upon war, the church lost its community in Indonesia. Buildings, including two churches, were destroyed completely; others were damaged and needed rebuilding. During and after the war there was opportunity to nurture intercommunion with Anglicans. It was of course thought unsatisfactory that Anglicans practised largely on Reformed church premises. Links with other Old Catholic provinces (excepting the Swiss) became difficult on political grounds. It needed time to return to normal. Communal suffering in the Dutch Church, as elsewhere, itself promoted ecumenical bonds. Relations with the Roman Catholic Church, which since the Second Vatican Council were in practice equivalent to intercommunion (in Rotterdam, for example) rose to a peak. In Holland today, there are about ten thousand Old Catholics.

The German church had to face special problems. After decades of suffering the disfavour of the authorities, it was treated by the National Socialist government exactly like other churches. This made expansion possible, but also presented the danger (true of all churches) of being infected with a novel political slant. Bishop Erwin Kreuzer of Bonn, and a majority of clergy, resisted this temptation. Many Old Catholic laity and clergy lost their lives; most churches were destroyed or severely damaged. However, the work of reconstruction was impressive. One notes in passing that where new churches were built, their architecture expressed no specifically Old Catholic character.[2] In the German Democratic Republic the position remains oppressive to the present day. Today, the German Church numbers over twenty thousand Old Catholic adherents. It endured, nevertheless, a powerful backlash when reinforced by Sudeten Germans exiled from Czechoslovakia.

In Austria, Old Catholicism was oppressed materially and spiritually during the War, under crippling political pressure. Even so, the outward effects of war were not altogether bad. From 1942 to 1949 the church was without a bishop. From 1945, religious education, the free press and parish life all had to be restarted. Now the church has some twenty-five thousand members. Within the last quarter of a century, retreat houses, geriatric and nursing homes, church centres and youth clubs have arisen in Holland, Switzerland, Germany and Austria. Until the War, the Old Catholic Church in Czechoslovakia consisted of thirteen predominantly German-speaking parishes, and one Czech parish. Later, the majority of the German-speaking inhabitants had to leave Czechoslovakia, including about twenty-four thousand Old Catholics. Small groups migrated to Austria, but the majority went to Germany to strengthen existing parishes. New parishes were also founded, as for example in northern Hesse, the Hartz, Saxony, and in Kaufbeuren, Rosenheim, Würzburg and Bayreuth. In Czechoslovakia the church dwindled to some four thousand souls. Its bishop Alois Pasček died in 1946. Not until 1968 could the church find a successor in Bishop Augustin Podolak, who shortly after was no longer permitted, for political reasons, to exercise office.

The Old Catholics of Yugoslavia, who are reputed to have numbered sixty thousand before the War, have since diminished to ten thousand. Of these, however, only four thousand belong to the Union of Utrecht, the Croat Old Catholics. In 1933 there was only one Old Catholic body in Yugoslavia. Its bishop, Marko Kalogjera,[3] was excluded from the Union of Utrecht the same year, by the International Conference of Old Catholic Bishops.[4] Most of the faithful remained loyal to him. However, one group separated in order to remain in the Union of Utrecht. In 1974 both groups were reunited. After the War, the church had reorganized itself into three parts (Croat, Slovene, Serb), each with its own bishop. Only the Croat diocese became a member of the Utrecht Union again in 1959.

The three churches combined in 1965, in a federation of autonomous Catholic churches of Yugoslavia. This federation did not alter
relations with Utrecht. Only the Croat Bishop Vilim Hušzak (1962–
1974) belonged to the Union of Utrecht and also to the federation.
Even now the *IBK* desires the three churches to unite, a hope which
probably misses the reality of their ethnic differences. Today there is
no Old Catholic bishop in Yugoslavia.[5]

In Paris, the sole French Old Catholic parish experienced great
difficulties during the War. Since 1951, there again existed a French
mission, at present with three priests recognized by the *IBK*.

Spared by the War, the Church in Switzerland evolved more
calmly. Even so, the membership continued to decline there too.
Today, Switzerland has fewer than twenty thousand Old Catholics.

In Italy, following the failure of early efforts in the wake of the
First Vatican Council, an Old Catholic community arose, recognized
after 1924 by the Swiss Bishop Adolf Küry. Since the mid 1960s there
were new efforts to call the Old Catholic mission to life. It was long
supported by the Swiss Church, but up to date has evolved no clear
form.

A high-church Lutheran episcopal group in Sweden was accepted
into the Union of Utrecht in 1976. One priest and two deacons were
ordained. The *IBK* placed this church under the authority of the
German bishop.

In other parts of this book appear comments on the churches in
Poland and North America. Here let it be noted that a mission was
founded (from North America) in Brazil. This mission was recognized unanimously by the *IBK* in 1978.

In general, the number of Old Catholics in Europe decreased.
Heavy losses arose directly as a consequence of the War, but a steady
decrease was to be observed later, too. The reasons are various.
More than ever, Old Catholics now live scattered abroad. In a
diaspora, loyalty to the church is more greatly endangered than with
a minority church enjoying state and national connections. Ecumenical familiarity, already long experienced, has since brought far fewer
participants into the partnership. Moreover, Old Catholic self-
consciousness was imprinted with a hostility to Rome, so that the
development of the Old Catholic churches following the Second
Vatican Council brought for many a sense of uncertainty. Finally, the
modern predilection for having smaller families is significant, as is

perhaps the less important trend towards leaving the church. If in Holland and Switzerland, despite these developments, the succession of priests from the ranks has generally been adequate, that is a matter for rejoicing.

It is also most fortunate that Bishop Urs Küry's characterization of the post-war period indicates both ecumenical action and theological reflection. Ecumenical endeavours are dealt with elsewhere in this book. It was of great significance that Küry traced this theology to the influence of Karl Barth on the Old Catholic Theological Faculty in the University of Berne. Even if the reaction to this influence is allowed for, the view is valid. Such a reaction demanded a review of the assumptions of the Old Catholic founding fathers. According to the views of Swiss Old Catholics influenced by Karl Barth, the founding fathers belonged all too greatly to the liberal Catholic theology of the nineteenth century. Their endeavours were based upon the contemplation of religion as the purely human possibility of climbing up to God. On the other hand, they wanted to testify to God's being 'vertically above',[6] in his omnipotent and merciful relation to man and the world. Thus they highlighted God's greatness, majesty and glory. This was regarded as a 'Copernican revolution' in the thinking of their time.

It is therefore not surprising if, at the first Old Catholic Congress after the War, at Hilversum in 1948, the Swiss Church and its theological faculty at Berne came under suspicion of 'protestantizing'. It is interesting that the Swiss, who recognized themselves as opponents of liberalism, were suspect precisely on account of their Barthian influence. This is not the contradiction it might seem, if it be considered that Barthianism could induce the same effect as the liberal (or rather, the idealist) Catholicism of the Old Catholic founders. These idealistic Catholics had little sympathy for the spirituality of the people. Pejoratives like 'popular Catholicism, superstition and uncouthness' came to them readily. Had these professorial postures continued to be influential, it is well known how they might have rendered ecclesiastical usage meaningless. In the face of the ideal God, whether or not as high above as the transcendent God of Barth, all kinds of things were placed in context as merely human. This stance was strengthened by the new transcendent theology. It also rendered pastoral care for souls more difficult, yet the common faithful could not be taken seriously as the bearers of the Holy Spirit. The theologian identified unwillingly with the élite, and thereby stood aloof by his authoritarian proclamation. The communal, brotherly, synodal system, demanded both by the liberals – not merely as a protest against the ultramontane system – and also by the Barthians, was thus rendered more complex. Mistrust of the Swiss led to the establishment of Old Catholic Theological Conferences, which is above all what the Dutch wished for.

They had at their disposal a relatively young and spiritually motivated clergy, and were no longer the reactionaries they were thought to be. However, they emerged from the Rinkel[7] school filled with a new Old Catholic consciousness. Now they showed themselves to be the motivating radicals. They worried greatly that paths trodden by sister churches of the Old Catholic heritage would alienate them. Wisely, however, they initiated the first study conference, not with purely theoretical discussion of Old Catholic existence and purpose. They proceeded pragmatically in the sense that after the clearing of some basic ecclesiological questions, they gave priority to problems of sacramental practice. It ought thus to be clear how far the participants. in catholic terms, were thinking specifically in *Old* Catholic terms.[8]

Meanwhile, the Dutch were also infected with the aforementioned 'transcendent' thinking. This concept strengthened an authoritarian stance of the kind evolved from pre-1870, or even 1721![9] Whereas at the time, ultramontanism could represent itself obviously as grand, Catholic liberalism, in keeping with its drive towards breadth and openness, found it harder to present so grand an ecclesiastical profile. Its openness to modernism and to contemporary spiritual currents rather concealed the danger of falling prey to secularizing tendencies. The new unclerical evaluation of the laity enhanced this danger. In addition, the struggle for a new concept of ministry and particularly of the episcopal office, was profoundly influenced by opposition to the ultramontane standpoint, to which positive alternatives were not yet clear. This may have been a reason why, after 1970, no bishop supported the conservative Old Catholic side.

Fear of clericalism, among liberals, was conducive to a separation (in homiletics) between the truth of the proclamation and the person of the preacher, which was not far different from the Barthian situation. Once the theologian is released from ecclesiastical authority, and the non-theologian delivered into the hands of the experts (without experiencing the truth in friendship and communion, personally) the effects are contradictory. Truth separated from its herald becomes depersonalized. It is also disconnected from the hearer of the proclamation. Whilst objectively true in itself, it is not integrated into the fellowship of the church. If, however, the theologian is at the same time a bishop – very often so with Old Catholics – an ecclesial structure arises very similar to the ultramontane. The genuine Old Catholic desire for synodical church structure must fall short in this respect, since everyone is accepted as a vehicle of the Holy Spirit and regarded as interdependent.

A communal view of the church is possible only if it is believed that God dwells within it and its members, and not merely far off and above all; not only *ultra montes* but *hic et nunc*. A fellowship without tangible communion remains an abstraction. Fellowship is concrete only where the parish recognizes in its bishops, priests and deacons, ambassadors of Christ, and where the ministry perceives the parishioners as bearers of the Holy Spirit. It was really the absorption of the tangible life of faith into the fellowship, reinforced by the Barthian influence, which evoked challenge to renewal, prompting the discovery of the new possibility of Eucharistic teaching in the 'local' Eucharist. Old Catholicism could be understood as a confession of the tangible presence of Christ in the church, *hic et nunc*.

Reference to the doctrine of the local church,[10] combined with the insight rejecting the *Filioque*, has facilitated a synodical ecclesiology. The doctrines of fellowship in God and fellowship in the church cannot be separated. The *Filioque* is possible only against the background of a more or less concealed concept of subordination, which has consequences in the concepts of both God and the church.

Elements which have led to this new understanding are of a different order: partly contemporary thought on the church, and partly practical theology. The *hic et nunc* has generally become more intensive. Further the abstract nature of theology, supported by Barth, urged people towards a new emphasis in the concrete. In non-ecclesiastical circles also, in industry for example, there is currently much in the way of a synodical approach to team decision-making and the nurture of interpersonal relationships. Influences of an 'interior theological' type are also significant, such as the Protestant K. L. Schmidt, or of the Orthodox Afanassieff.

If the Old Catholic Congresses, just like the International Old Catholic Theological Conferences, turned from the mode of listening to lectures, and increasingly favoured group-work, this probably did not occur under the impact of the modern crisis of faith, as Urs Küry's last pastoral letter suggested. Rather, it was the fruit of a theological reorientation towards incarnation and pneumatology, which increasingly characterized the themes of the 1960s and after. The rise of confraternities in various countries, and the enthusiasm with which churches now strive for renewal, correspond to this interpretation. So today church renewal, such as that attempted through group concerns, as far as possible involves the wider social circle. This is true, for example, in Switzerland, of liturgical revision, where, in principle, every member may participate in the reshaping of the constitution and religious education, and in the deepening of pastoral care. As far as themes of theological conferences are concerned, the contemporary trend is indicated in the following examples: the Old Catholic Congress of 1952 instructed on repentance, church and bible; that of 1974 followed the theme of life; that of 1978 the understanding of the Trinity by the world and the church (all of which took place in group discussions). The Theological Conference of 1962 consisted predominantly of talks about justification and salvation; that of 1978 worked in groups on the variety of pastoral counselling conducted on the basis of participants' recorded memories.[11]

Reflection upon the synodical character of the church, complete in every episcopal communion, has made it possible to rethink relationships with Rome. In 1950, the *IBK* protest against the dogmatization of the Assumption of the Virgin Mary was still regarded as quite anti-Roman, being formulated in such a way as to render undue support for the anti-Catholic opinion that this pious belief (that Mary was bodily assumed) deserved utter condemnation. Even so, two developments around 1970 made possible a freer stance *vis-à-vis* Rome. First was the aforementioned resumption of the original Old Catholic episcopal-synodical concept of the church. Secondly were those developments in the Roman Catholic Church consequent upon the Second Vatican Council. The former development arrived officially in the 'Declaration of the Old Catholic Bishops, of 18 July 1970, on Primacy in the Church'. The changed attitude of Rome, in Holland, Germany and Switzerland, has made possible official conversations between the two churches.

In Holland on 7 November 1966, it was possible for Augustine Cardinal Bea[12] to declare that the prior attitude of Rome in permitting no dialogue with Old Catholic clergy (so long as the latter had not signed the 'Formulary of Alexander VII' and the Bull *Unigenitus*) had been superseded. Permission was given by Rome in 1968 to have conversations in the three countries, about mutual pastoral and sacramental help in borderline cases. In each country a special text was worked out – having the same essential content – by which each church was to make a declaration about this ministry. Given papal approval, the two Dutch churches were able to validate their declarations. As to publication, however, they continued to wait until the same was possible in Germany and Switzerland. It is worthy of mention that in Switzerland the Old Catholic side twice asked all its parish councils for opinion about the proposed text.

On the basis of this novel situation, the International Old Catholic Theological Conference of 1969 was able to suggest positively what an acknowledgement of the historical primacy of the papacy would signify. It drew the conclusion that the New Testament bears witness to the Petrine office, that this office remains even today (because church structure is still moulded upon it), and that despite all the disagreeable developments of the past, leading to various schisms such as that of Utrecht, it is still possible to view acceptance of the papal office as a symbol of the function which Rome began to fulfil in the history of the church. Papacy contains not only 'primarily legal authority, but obligation, like the duty of taking initiatives in the cause of unity, and if required, the pronouncement of the church's judgment on common problems. This fact tacitly repudiates the notion that Rome has the conclusive say on such matters. The *IBK* Declaration of 1970 intended to convey just such ideas.

By comparison with the Roman Catholic Church in the same countries, the Old Catholic churches of central Europe today are reactionary and conservative. Partly they understand this tendency within themselves as a waning of the earlier desire for progress. The trend, as such, is regretted, whilst in certain other respects it is nurtured and desired.

How much has Barthianism, which was hailed at first as a new lease of life, had the effect of disturbing Old Catholic ecclesiastical life? This becomes clear when we see how the new resolutions about intercommunion came into being. These resolutions, concluded in Vienna on 21 September 1965, with the autonomous Catholic churches of the Philippines, Spain and Portugal, were moulded upon the Bonn Agreement of 1931. These new treaties were arranged only because bishops and theologians were under less constraint to remain silent. At the Old Catholic Congress on the day after the Treaty was publicised, Curé Léon Gauthier[13] protested against this procedure as involving the exclusion of the churches. His protest was accepted only years later via an Orthodox article in the Old Catholic press. Out of sight of modern Old Catholic self-awareness, the entire procedure appears incomprehensible. It also contradicts the thinking of the Old Catholic fathers.

Preparation of the resolutions on intercommunion by the *IBK* occurred largely in conjunction with Anglican advisers, especially where the Philippines Independent Church was concerned. This church was scarcely known at all, as becomes clear from the report of the *IKZ* 1964, Number 2. Thus intercommunion with this body has remained without practical significance until this day. Things were rather different with the Spanish and Portuguese, since Old Catholic bishops had been practising intercommunion for some time previous to the resolution, and had even participated in the consecrations of bishops. In their day, Bishops Reinkens and Herzog had behaved similarly, long before 1931, towards Anglican churches – though never at episcopal consecrations – but those were the days of ecumenical pioneering. The bishops had acted as representatives of their churches, and not secretly.

Such events had made it clear that the Utrecht Union of 1889, which experienced an unpublicized reform in 1952, required complete overhaul. Reorganization was set in motion on 12 September 1974, and published in that year's *IKZ*[14]. The statement also contained an enactment about doctrine, whereby the Declaration of Utrecht, 1889, was ratified, and in which the basis of the community of bishops and their churches in the Union of Utrecht, and the catholicity of their office and worship, were set forth. It should be noticed that the Declaration of Utrecht had previously been ratified in that, in negotiations with the Orthodox in 1931, the number 'seven' was stipulated in connection with 'authoritative councils'.[15] The encyclical of the 1970 *IBK* confirmed this.

The revised union provides, among other things, for relations with other churches. An Old Catholic province may not be responsible alone, but only through the *IBK* collectively, as seen in the practical issue of the consecrations of bishops for churches not belonging to the Utrecht Union or in communion with it. Such a case, already adverted to, happened when two Old Catholic bishops participated in the consecration of a Lusitanian bishop by an Anglican in 1962. The question is open as to what kind of ecclesiastical agreement stands behind such a transaction and underlies the prevailing rules.

On this basis, it should be recognized that the decisions of the *IBK*, via the individual bishops in their sees, were to be executed within the framework of contemporary ecclesiastical polity. In declarations of faith and order bishops must act in agreement with their churches.

The ordinance resolving this principle was not observed two years later, when the *IBK* on 7 December 1976, issued its second declaration on the subject of the ordination of women. In a former declaration of April 1972, the *IBK* prohibited the ministry of women ordained to Anglican orders, within Old Catholic churches. The 1976 declaration refused, 'in agreement with the ancient undivided church', the sacramental ordination of women to the catholic, apostolic offices of deacon, priest and bishop. The Declaration stated:

The question of the ordination of women touches upon the basic ordering of and the mystery of the church.

At the same time, however, it saw the possibility that this question would be discussed further.[16] The *IBK* had previously asked the Old Catholic seminaries for expert opinion, but had then taken scant notice of this, and had acted without recognizable consideration for agreement within their churches.

Concerning the possibility of further discussion of the ordination of women, the national synod of the Swiss Old Catholic Church asked the *IBK* in 1981 to examine the question of admitting women to the diaconate. However, an individual Old Catholic province, that of North America in fact, damaged the Union of Utrecht, when Prime Bishop Thaddeus Zielinski,[17] late in 1976, abrogated intercommunion with the Episcopal Church until the following synod. This act must of course be seen in connection with the method by which intercommunion had first been adopted.

Intercommunion between American Old Catholics and Episcopalians raises two questions, both in view of the agreement and its ultimate abrogation. A treaty was not made until long after 1931, and therefore not automatically in concert with other churches of the Union of Utrecht, even though two American bishops and other Old Catholic bishops had signed the 1931 Agreement. North American intercommunion was not ratified until the General Synod at Scranton in October 1946. The Bonn Agreement was thereby clarified in a declaration prepared by representatives of both American churches. The following statement is of special interest:

The reception of the blessed sacrament by believers of the Polish National Catholic Church in the Episcopal Church and vice-versa is permitted only in urgent cases or with the agreement of the bishops concerned.

In general, such a reception procedure would be validated positively only by agreement among the Old Catholic churches, and then in view of the results. Each church has to accept entirely (in obedience to its bishops rather than by following its resolutions) what it recognizes as valid. Of course it is regrettable that the American development was not recognized by the European churches. Any reception procedure would have had to wait until all Old Catholic and Anglican churches were united on it. In principle, these reflections are valid also for the rescinding of intercommunion, in which connection it may be said that the debate about ordination of women was taken seriously only in America, in that only there did an official mixed Anglican and Old Catholic commission discuss the problem. Unfortunately, this fact may be cited only if it is also admitted that the American Old Catholics acted questionably in relation to their Anglican brethren. This is so because the commission claimed that ordination of women was merely an internal question for Anglicans, which need have no effect upon intercommunion. When, however, Episcopalians allowed women to be ordained, there was opposition to it.

The German Old Catholic Pastoral Conference of 1977 was of the opinion that intercommunion with Anglicans could not be questioned with reference to the ordination of women. Likewise, in April 1977, a free Anglican-Old Catholic conference of theologians in Chichester discussed this question at the request of the Archbishop of Canterbury.[18] No noteworthy results were achieved. On neither side has the question been exhausted thoroughly. The Old Catholics themselves were not prepared (inasmuch as individual theologians had concerned themselves with the matter) to discuss this thorny issue on a universal Catholic basis. The International Old Catholic Theological Conference of 1971 listened to a short lecture directed to the position of the Anglican churches. In 1970, the *IBK* had established a commission for the study of this question, but supported it so poorly that it was unable to convene on any single occasion! All that remained was a scanty correspondence.

Upon this problem a few particular remarks are necessary. If the life of faith in the intellectual tradition suffers a disturbed relationship with the non-rational stratum of human nature, it is not easy to see that theological arguments exist against ordaining women to the priesthood or episcopate. For within the intellect are scarcely manifest differences between the sexes. It would appear somewhat artificial to ask whether the sexual differentiation (which for God the creator is central) must not also be sacred within the Redeemer, whose holiness finds expression at the core of the church, in the celebration of the Eucharist. Traditionally this expression has been precise owing to the fact that only men have been able to preside at the Eucharist. Added to the intellectual tradition is the modern intuition that the parish is of secondary importance to the priest. This implies discrimination against the woman if she cannot ascend to the first rank. The question emerges as to whether both difficulties may not be merged, and whether emphasis upon the intellect cannot go with the neglect of the Holy Spirit. Were the Holy Spirit taken more seriously for his omnipresent divinity, it would no longer be comprehensible that a layman − man or woman − would be of secondary importance in the priest's eyes. Indeed, every Christian is a bearer of the Holy Spirit.

A commission of the Swiss Church has concerned itself with the question of the relationship of man and woman in the church, and in connection with the ministerial offices of the church, since 1979.

The meeting of the Anglican-Old Catholic Theological Commission in 1977 was the sixth since 1946. Of course it is necessary that such commissions meet more frequently and also at the official level. The 1931 Bonn Agreement has, to date, never been thought through by both sides in order to examine its implications. It took effect upon an unsatisfactory basis. With this in mind, the *IBK* was invited to express its attitudes to the church union scheme in South India and Sri Lanka, in North India and Pakistan, and concerning Anglican negotiations with the Methodists. On the other hand, Old Catholics have never invited Anglican churches to offer their opinions, particularly on the important question of the *Filioque* from a dogmatic standpoint. Without consultation with Anglicans, Old Catholic bishops determined this matter of faith, in 1970, rather than merely the legality or otherwise of its insertion into the Credo.

As an effect of intercommunion the support of Anglican missionary bishoprics in Africa needs mention. This represents almost the sole Old Catholic effort in the department of foreign missions.[19]

The declaration of 1970 on the *Filioque* was made in conjunction with a newly arranged dialogue with the Orthodox. In the same year and similar circumstances, the *IBK* promulgated a 'pastoral letter', in which it professed the doctrine of the local church, and rejected every theological doctrine which made the Son joint origin (with the Father) of the Holy Spirit.

Consequent upon the third Pan-Orthodox Conference at Rhodes, a mixed Orthodox and Old Catholic dialogue was instituted, which in 1975, after preparatory sessions, met officially for the first time. It worked on common texts about the dominant areas in theology, special weight being given to ecclesiology. The parties have taken up clear positions in respect of these texts, and the commission's work is to examine the standpoints taken. After completion of work on the texts, the churches will then have to decide whether they can declare themselves fully and mutually as Catholic churches, and whether they can and must enter into full communion. Negotiations both with Rome and Orthodoxy will be discussed through the International Old Catholic Theological Conference and in wider circles.

As far as relations with Rome are concerned, it was sufficient in the first decades of the Old Catholic movement, for the conversion of a Roman Catholic priest to Old Catholicism, that he deny the First Vatican Council. More recently, and rather more consciously today, a thoroughgoing period of training is required.

The Old Catholic Communion has also been confronted with a case of heresy. A German priest and former professor living in retirement, who had already published several theological articles, in 1980 directed an attack in the *IKZ*[20] against the fundamental dogmas of the Church. His bishop reacted, together with the college of university doctors and the clergy conference, in the following issue.[21] This rejoinder maintained that the critical piece in question did not correspond with Old Catholic doctrine, and (considering the great age of the author) that the attack was solely an academic one, to which the bishop now argued a corrective reply.

The impetus of the early days is missing from Old Catholicism. Apart from exceptions, such as the 'Apostoleia' community, founded in Holland in 1942 for home missions, very little effort is taken for the propagation of the Old Catholic faith. Furthermore, resources for such needs are lacking. Work in the diaspora lays claim to more and more energy, as do solutions to internal problems and intensive ecumenical responsibilities. Repeatedly, therefore, feelings of frustration arise, with the consequent temptation to attitudes of resignation. The effects are obvious. Despondency cannot be overcome by the temptation to extol our merits. It is more a question, assuming that we are convinced of the significance of the Old Catholic position, to think this position through more completely, and to live it more thoroughly.

NOTES

1. Bishop in Berne, 1955–72; son of Adolf Küry, bishop since 1924.
2. In Switzerland also, the first Old Catholic building on their own account (Lucerne, 1890), no ultramontane predilection for the neo-Gothic was followed; instead they imitated the early Christian basilica. Later building simply emulated contemporary styles.
3. A canon of Split (Croatia) consecrated, 1924, in Utrecht by Archbishop Kenninck.
4. Internationale Altkatholische Bischofskonferenz (*IBK*).
5. No successor was appointed to Huszak, who died in 1974. The region is usually administered from Bonn.
6. The German phrase, 'Senkrecht von oben', implies a view of the transcendent nature of God, after the Hegelian concept.
7. Andreas Rinkel, Archbishop of Utrecht, 1937–70.
8. Urs Küry in *Internationale Kirchliche Zeitschrift (IKZ)*, 1977, p. 141.
9. Arguably the year of the greatest theological unrest following the Bull *Unigenitus* (1713), when Quesnel's 'Propositions' were translated into English and other languages; virtually the watershed of Jansenism in Holland.
10. 'Ortskirchenlehre', local ecclesiology.
11. In Anglo-American parlance called 'non-directive' counselling.
12. Head of the Vatican Secretariat for promoting Christian Unity.
13. Now bishop of the Swiss province called the Christkatholischeskirche. His protest was that the 'local' churches seemed to have no part in decision-making over this matter.
14. pp. 224 ff.
15. The Union of Utrecht categorically acknowledges the authority of the first seven General Councils of the Church.
16. One of the bishops voted against the Declaration; the first case in which the *IBK* did not act unanimously.
17. Primate of the Polish National Catholic Church (PNCC) of North America.
18. Dr. Donald Coggan.
19. The PNCC has also supported an Anglican mission in Belize.

20. F. P. Pfister, *Was wollte die Katholisch-Nationalkirchliche Bewegung (KNB) im Dritten Reich?*, *IKZ* vol. 1, 1980.
21. *IKZ* vol. 2, 1980.

4

Variations on an Old Catholic Theme: The Polish National Catholic Church

Laurence Orzell

The word 'paradox' perhaps best characterizes the Polish experience of Old Catholicism. The very fact that the numerically largest Old Catholic Churches – the Polish National Catholic Church of America and the Polish Catholic Church of Poland – arose among a people known throughout history for their devotion to the Roman Church is in itself a paradox. Paradoxical also is the fact that these churches originally emerged not as a result of doctrinal disagreements but rather because of administrative difficulties among Polish Roman Catholic immigrants in the United States at the turn of the century. And when a minority within the Polish minority in America did break with Rome, its subsequent doctrinal development followed paths that did not invariably correspond to those established by European Old Catholics.

At the same time, the Polish participants in the Old Catholic movement have had much in common with their Western European brothers: above all their opposition to papal claims and a positive attitude toward Anglicanism. Even here, though, we cannot escape a paradox. While Polish Old Catholics attempted to establish intercommunion with Anglicans nearly thirty years before similar attempts bore fruit at Bonn, it was the Polish National Catholic Church which found it necessary in the 1970s to terminate this relationship with American Episcopalians. And even this arose out of yet another paradox, for while liberal – and even radical – theological trends characterized the Polish National Catholic Church during much of its early history, recent years have witnessed a marked shift towards a more conservative attitude in questions of faith and order. Yet throughout their turbulent past, Polish National

Catholics have remained loyal to the Union of Utrecht and have valued their membership in a communion dedicated to the preservation of the faith practised in the Undivided Church.

Promising Starts, False Hopes

The period 1880–1914 witnessed a massive migration of Poles from their partitioned homeland to the United States. Adjustment to an alien social and economic environment proved difficult, and the frustration felt by these immigrants erupted in the religious arena. The American Roman Catholic hierarchy, composed almost exclusively of bishops of Irish descent, permitted the establishment of Polish parishes but regarded these as a purely temporary phenomenon and favoured instead the 'Americanization' of the immigrants. The hierarchy's generally negative attitude towards Polish language and culture clashed with the views of those Poles who nurtured a strong sense of their ethnic identity. This philosophical conflict translated itself into calls on the part of some immigrant laity for a greater role in the administration of parish affairs. Moreover, these Poles called for the appointment of Polish bishops. Neither Rome nor the American hierarchy paid much attention to these demands, and open dissent – in the form of schism – became all but inevitable.[1]

The first significant schism of this nature and the one which gave rise to the establishment of a legitimate Old Catholic Church in America occurred among the Poles of Chicago during 1895. The members of St. Hedwig's parish alleged that their pastor, Fr. Joseph Barzynski, had mismanaged their affairs and asked that his assistant, Fr. Anthony Kozlowski, assume charge of the church. Fr. Kozlowski, born in Russian Poland during 1857 and ordained at Taranto, Italy, in 1885, accepted the mantle of leadership proffered by the Poles. Yet neither he nor his followers received succour or sympathy from Archbishop Patrick Feehan of Chicago. They then took their case to the Apostolic Delegate, Archbishop Francis Satolli, with much the same result. But the dissident Poles decided to resist, and violent demonstrations broke out in February 1895. Archbishop Feehan removed Fr. Barzynski but replaced him with another priest when the dissidents refused to accept. The Poles had little recourse, however, for under the terms of canon law as practised in America, Archbishop Feehan held legal title to St. Hedwig's parish.[2]

By May 1895 Fr. Kozlowski and his flock concluded that they

must needs opt for one of two alternatives: submission to the archbishop or the establishment of a new parish, Catholic in faith and practice but independent of archiepiscopal jurisdiction. They chose the latter and began to construct a new church, All Saints' parish, which Fr. Kozlowski blessed on 11 August of that year. Archbishop Feehan excommunicated the Polish priest on 29 September, but Fr. Kozlowski and his adherents remained adamant.[3] Initially, the chief *raison d'être* of All Saints' parish was congregational ownership of ecclesiastical property and lay management of church finances. With this one difference, the 'Independents' – as they sometimes called themselves – were basically Roman Catholic in belief. This arrangement proved satisfactory to many discontented Poles, and a number of similar congregations sprang up, some of which came to accept Fr. Kozlowski as their spiritual leader.

The subsequent spread of the 'Independent' movement and a realization that the profession of Roman Catholicism outside the Roman Church was untenable persuaded Fr. Kozlowski to establish a formal ecclesiastical alternative for dissident Poles. Elected bishop by his supporters, he approached the Old Catholics for consecration. Following an investigation, the Old Catholics responded positively. Fr. Kozlowski accepted the Declaration of Utrecht and received episcopal ordination in Berne on 21 November 1897 at the hands of Bishop Eduard Herzog, with the assistance as co-consecrators of Archbishop Gerard Gul and Bishop Theodore Weber. Upon his return, Bishop Kozlowski proceeded to consolidate what he called the 'Polish Catholic Church'; he also used the term 'Independent Catholic Diocese of Chicago'. In a pastoral letter he openly criticized the 'religious despotism' of the Roman Church, but he concomitantly emphasized that 'you neither intended to form a new religion or new creeds, nor to reject the faith, which was transmitted to you by your fathers'.[4] Clearly, the entire tenor of the document indicated that he had come to share principles held by European Old Catholics and by many Anglicans.

Affiliation with the Old Catholic movement did not prove an unmixed blessing for Bishop Kozlowski. Pope Leo XIII excommunicated him by name in April 1898, and this tended to retard his progress among the Poles. More important, however, was the fact that most immigrants regarded Old Catholicism as a German phenomenon and hence unacceptable to patriotic Poles. Indeed, General Alexander Kirejew, a Russian Orthodox friend of Old

Catholicism, openly suggested that Old Catholic ideas could serve to wean the Polish nation from Rome and render it amenable to domination by its partitioners.[5] Finally, the ecclesiastical mischief worked in America by an *episcopus vagans*, Archbishop Joseph René Vilatte, who falsely claimed Old Catholic status, tended to bring Old Catholicism into disrepute. For this reason both Roman Catholics and those dissidents who refused allegiance to the Polish Catholic Church labelled Bishop Kozlowski a traitor to Poland. Despite tremendous odds, however, the church attained no small measure of success. In 1898 it conducted a synod in Chicago at which the delegates adopted a constitution that enshrined the principle of lay participation in church management and pledged allegiance to several Old Catholic ideas, particularly those concerning the papacy; however, the Polish Catholic Church continued to accept the dogma of the Immaculate Conception and to utilize Latin as a liturgical language. Moreover, Bishop Kozlowski drew up ambitious plans for the construction of a hospital in Chicago and periodically attempted to unite all Polish dissidents under his wing. These plans came to nought, as did his most ambitious proposal: the establishment of intercommunion with the Episcopal Church.[6]

Bishop Kozlowski's desire for intercommunion arose from three principal factors: his friendship with Charles Grafton, Episcopal Bishop of Fond du Lac, Wisconsin; his belief that the Polish Catholic Church required both material and spiritual assistance; and support for such a move on the part of Bishop Herzog. Bishop Grafton, a leading Anglo-Catholic, entertained a very high opinion of the Polish prelate and invited him to participate in the consecration of a coadjutor at Fond du Lac in 1900. Strong opposition from several Episcopal bishops, who considered the Pole a 'schismatic', prevented this, but Bishop Grafton saw in the Polish church a means to strengthen Anglo-Catholicism and concomitantly to repair some of the damage done by Archbishop Vilatte. He thus encouraged Bishop Kozlowski to request formal recognition from and intercommunion with Episcopalians. The Polish prelate consequently submitted a 'Memorial' to the General Convention of the Episcopal Church at San Francisco in October 1901. He based this request on the Lambeth Quadrilateral (1888) and asked 'to be admitted to your Christian fellowship and Communion'. By implication he rejected the dogma of the Immaculate Conception, noted that his church would adopt a vernacular liturgy and claimed the allegiance of twenty-six priests, twenty-five parishes and 80,000 souls. In effect, the 'Memorial' proposed a type of affiliation that went beyond intercommunion in that its terms were tantamount to the creation of an autonomous Polish jurisdiction within the Episcopal Church.[7]

The General Convention remanded the 'Memorial' to a committee for study, but no action followed. Bishop Kozlowski returned to the charge in 1902 with much the same result. Apparently, a reluctance openly to affiliate with a group which differed so much in religious, social and economic background, as well as the belief that the consecration of the Polish prelate in some way infringed upon their jurisdiction, bulked large as reasons for what Bishop Grafton subsequently termed the 'scant courtesy' with which Episcopal hierarchs handled the matter. At a special meeting of Episcopal bishops in October 1902 the prelates extended 'their Christian salutations and assurances of affectionate sympathy' but refused to grant any recognition. Moreover, they once again relegated the request to a committee for further study.[8]

Encouraged by Bishop Grafton, who helped him draft a constitution and statement of faith that brought the Polish Catholic Church into greater accord with Anglicanism, Bishop Kozlowski sought support from several Episcopal prelates, including Dr. Henry Potter, Bishop of New York. The Polish bishop and one of his priests, Fr. T. Jakimowicz, addressed the Church Club, an Episcopal organization, in New York on 25 February 1903 and renewed the Polish Catholic petition. Those in attendance gave the Poles a warm reception but made it clear that any merger between the Polish Catholic and Episcopal Churches must needs be 'temporary', pending the assimilation of the Poles into existing Episcopal dioceses.[9]

This lack of tangible results no doubt discouraged Bishop Kozlowski, but he resolved to carry on alone. He attended an Old Catholic meeting in Switzerland during 1904 and unsuccessfully promoted the consecration of one of his clergymen, Fr. John Francis Tichy, a Czech. Illness, financial difficulties and feuding among the dissident Poles took their toll on the prelate, and he declined markedly. By the close of 1906 most of his parishes had collapsed or had affiliated with a more dynamic dissident group based in Pennsylvania. On 14 January 1907 Bishop Kozlowski died at Chicago without nominating any agreed successor. On this uncertain note closed the first major attempt to organize an Old Catholic Church in America.[10]

A Surer Foundation

As mentioned above, not all Polish dissidents accepted the jurisdiction of Bishop Kozlowski. By 1907 many had affiliated with another organization, commonly called the 'Polish National Church', which had emerged at Scranton, Pennsylvania in 1897. The origins of this group paralleled those of the Polish Catholic Church. Dissatisfied members of Scranton's Sacred Hearts of Jesus and Mary parish pressed for the removal of their pastor, Fr. Richard Aust, and a small-scale riot ensued on 6 September 1896. Fr. Aust's removal by the diocesan ordinary, Bishop William O'Hara, failed to satisfy the Poles. They proceeded to construct a new church, St. Stanislaus parish, and offered the pastorate to Fr. Francis Hodur, who previously had served as Fr. Aust's assistant. In March 1897 Fr. Hodur joined his new flock and incurred ecclesiastical suspension.[11]

Thus far the Scranton group differed little from that at Chicago. It nonetheless gradually became apparent that the Scranton dissidents would adopt a different tone. Fr. Hodur, born in Austrian Poland during 1866 and ordained at Scranton in 1893, was a very complex man whose radical rhetoric blended populism, nationalism, anti-clericalism, Catholicism and, initially, socialism into an attractive and explosive mixture. At first he desired to create a 'National Church' in communion with Rome that would prevent the 'denationalization' of the Poles in the religious, economic and social spheres, and he propagated these ideas through his journal *Straz* (*The Guard*). In 1898 he journeyed to the Vatican and bore a petition which requested concessions for the immigrants on questions of parish administration and the nomination of a Polish bishop. Rome turned a deaf ear, and he was excommunicated on 29 September 1898.

Fr. Hodur's excommunication did not deter the determined priest. He openly denied papal infallibility and inveighed against the 'corruption' wrought by Rome over the centuries. Despite his often intemperate language, however, Fr. Hodur sought to preserve Catholicism outside the Roman fold. He and the few priests who followed him continued to celebrate mass in Latin, observe traditional Marian devotions and generally to hold to a Catholicism purged of perceived papal errors. Possessed by the belief that he alone could lead the Poles away from Rome, he distanced himself from Bishop Kozlowski and criticized the latter's policies. Nonetheless, the Scranton priest approached Archbishop Gul in January 1899 and requested consecration. Owing to Old Catholic reservations as to Fr. Hodur's relationship with the Chicago prelate, the archbishop did not respond positively. Nor did the Old Catholics alter their attitude when the Scranton priest, following a brief rapprochement with Bishop Kozlowski, returned to the charge in February 1900.

But Fr. Hodur persisted and proceeded to set up his Polish National Church independent of both Rome and the Chicago group. He proved hostile to Bishop Kozlowski's attemps to establish intercommunion with Episcopalians and instead emphasized the Polish nature of his organization. For example, he introduced the Polish language into the liturgy and celebrated a Polish mass at Christmas 1901. The vernacular, as well as Fr. Hodur's magnetic personality and energetic nature, did much to consolidate his group. By 1904 he claimed the allegiance of twelve parishes with 10,000 adherents. In September of that year he convened a synod which denounced papal infallibility. The delegates adopted a constitution for the organization, now also referred to as the 'Polish National Catholic Church', that established a quinquennial General Synod as the highest administrative authority. Parishes would enjoy considerable autonomy but owed 'obedience' to a bishop elected for life 'in questions of faith, morals and discipline'. The bishop nonetheless would govern in consultation with a Grand Council which included clergy and laity. To no one's surprise, the delegates elected Fr. Hodur bishop and went on record in favour of union with Bishop Kozlowski's adherents.

The prospects for the post-synodal period appeared bright but quickly faded. Fr. Hodur once again approached the Old Catholics for consecration, but the latter did not respond favourably, chiefly owing to what they subsequently termed the 'obscure relationship' between the Chicago and Scranton camps. A plan to unite the two factions received approval at a Polish Catholic synod in Chicago in late 1904, but this rapprochement quickly proved abortive. Moreover, Roman Catholic attacks and periodic rebellion in the ranks of his priests proved detrimental, and Fr. Hodur found himself forced to take drastic measures to secure competent clergy. Not all of these moves proved consistent with his avowed adherence to genuine Catholic teaching.

The entire situation altered upon the demise of Bishop Kozlowski in January 1907. The European Old Catholics advised the feuding Poles that they 'must be reconciled' because their 'disagreements are a scandal'. By July 1907 this prudent counsel bore fruit with the selection at Chicago of Fr. Hodur as the late bishop's successor, a choice ratified by a meeting of clergy from both groups at New York in early August. But one obstacle remained. Fr. Tichy, whose candidacy for the episcopate Bishop Kozlowski had unsuccessfully promoted in 1904, also petitioned the Old Catholics for consecration. Both he and Fr. Hodur appeared before the Old Catholic Congress at The Hague in September 1907, and each received a hearing. Fr. Hodur's arguments carried the day, for after some deliberation the European prelates resolved to elevate the Scranton priest. Fr. Hodur signed the Declaration of Utrecht, and 29 September 1907 – the ninth anniversary of his excommunication – he received the order of bishop from Archbishop Gul, assisted by Bishops James van Thiel and Nicholas Spit.

Organizational and Ideological Development

The consecration of Bishop Hodur supplied a sound basis for the further growth of the Polish National Catholic Church (hereafter abbreviated PNCC). Membership in the Old Catholic Communion ended the ecclesiastical isolation of the Polish church and gave it an unquestionable claim to Catholicity. And this growth initially weathered well the virtual cessation of Polish emigration to America following World War I, as well as the incessant anathemas heaped on Bishop Hodur by his enemies. In 1906 the church claimed twenty-four parishes with over 15,000 members. Ten years later the number of adherents had nearly tripled, and the PNCC by then comprised thirty-four congregations. The period 1916–26 constituted the church's greatest period of growth, for in the latter year it included ninety-one parishes with over 61,000 members. This development persisted, albeit at a slower pace, during the following decade. By 1936 the PNCC claimed 118 parishes. And along with growth came subdivision. In the years following the first consecration of bishops by the PNCC's leader in 1924, territorial reorganization into dioceses occurred: the Central Diocese (based in Scranton); the Eastern Diocese (based eventually in Manchester, New Hampshire); the Western Diocese (based in Chicago); and the Buffalo-Pittsburgh Diocese (based in Buffalo, New York). Bishop Hodur founded a fraternal insurance organization, the Polish National Union, in 1908 to help meet the material needs of his flock, and he began the publication of a bi-weekly organ, *Rola Boza (God's Field)* in 1923. Morevoer, work among other ethnic groups, primarily Lithuanians, began. And throughout this expansion the PNCC's organizer retained a strong hand as the church's 'Prime Bishop' until infirmities sapped his physical strength in the latter 1930s and 1940s.[12]

The post-1907 period of development also witnessed an evolution of Polish National Catholic doctrine and discipline that increasingly set it apart from both its Roman Catholic parent and its Old Catholic sister churches. Bishop Hodur continually criticized what he termed the 'medieval' understanding of Catholicism that obtained in the Roman Church. His reaction emerged most clearly in 1913 with the publication of a tract, *Our Faith*, a work which both reflected the influence of modernism and foreshadowed some views which would gain vogue later in the century. *Our Faith* constituted an elaboration of the PNCC's *Confession of Faith*, which received approval at a General Synod in 1914. The *Confession*, intended to supplement, not supplant, the Nicene Creed, could be interpreted as a reaffirmation of most cardinal Catholic dogmas, though traditional terminology was noticeably absent. And the *Confession* went beyond theology *per se* in that it stated 'that privileges arising from differences in rank, from possession of immense riches or from differences of faith, sex and race are a great wrong . . .'[13]

In *Our Faith* Bishop Hodur further elaborated on this curious combination of old and new. He stressed that the PNCC 'recognizes the same sacraments as the Roman Catholic, Eastern and Old Catholic Churches'. Yet, motivated by a fervent desire to bring renewed emphasis to Scripture, he numbered the 'Word of God' among the sacraments, because 'listening to the Word of God' draws man to his creator. Indeed, a General Synod in 1909 already had declared the 'Word of God' to be a sacrament but had preserved the traditional number of seven sacraments by listing together baptism and confirmation. The most conspicuous innovation of *Our Faith*, however, was the rejection of eternal punishment in favour of an apocatastatic theory of finite purgation. This innovation, to which Bishop Hodur added a radically modernistic concept of original sin, found still further expression in his *Eleven Great Principles* (1923) and in his mystical work *Apocalypse of the Twentieth Century* (1930). Other alterations adopted by the PNCC included the implementation for adults of general or corporate confession (1914) and the formal abolition of compulsory clerical celibacy (1921). Both of the latter practices had precedents within the European Old Catholic Churches.[14]

In any evaluation of Polish National Catholic doctrine, however, one should keep in mind that not all of Bishop Hodur's writings are considered normative for the PNCC. For example, the 'Foreword' to a translation of *Our Faith* published in the 1960s stated that the views contained therein do 'not constitute an official and final dogma of the Polish National Catholic Church's teaching...'[15] The bishop's primary concerns were pastoral and social rather than theological, and he wrote more to inspire action than to stimulate systematic theological speculation. Rather, in accordance with the adage *lex orandi, lex credendi*, one must needs take account of the everyday liturgical life of the PNCC. Here the church evinced a far less radical frame of mind. The sacrifice of the mass, offered for the living and the dead, remained essentially Tridentine in form and substance. Indeed, when Bishop Hodur in the 1930s attempted to introduce the celebration of mass facing the people and other liturgical changes, the majority of the clergy and laity demurred. Moreover, the PNCC adhered to the doctrine of the Real Presence, and observed much devotion to the Blessed Virgin.

The continued Catholic affinities of the PNCC also emerged in the ties maintained by Bishop Hodur with the European Old Catholics. Though he did not find it possible actively to participate in most sessions of the International Bishops' Conference, he did periodically attend, and he also sent representatives to meetings of the various Old Catholic Congresses. Basically, Bishop Hodur believed that the social and religious environment in which his church functioned necessitated a good measure of autonomy, both disciplinary and doctrinal. For example, when he appeared at a meeting of Old Catholic bishops in Cologne during 1913, he defended the PNCC's *Confession* as a necessary response to conditions in America and pledged that he held its terms merely as an 'opinion'. He also denied any intention to alter genuine Catholic dogma.[16] In subsequent years, the course of his doctrinal development and his nationalistic fervour created some anxiety in the minds of his European brothers, but they did not regard these as grounds for any formal action and tolerated his theological views as what they termed a *schola americana*. Moreover, they came to accept some of his actions – such as his consecration of four bishops in 1924 without assistance – as dictated by necessity. During a meeting with Archbishop Francis Kenninck, the latter told the Polish prelate, 'I do not envy you your position', and the Old Catholics consequently placed great trust in Bishop Hodur's judgement. This trust did not go unrequited, given the growth and vitality of the PNCC.[17]

The Polish church did not confine its ecumenical relations to the European Old Catholics but extended contacts to Episcopalians as well. In 1910 Bishop Grafton secured the appointment of an Episcopal committee to study the possibility of intercommunion with the Poles, but once again these plans came to nought. Cordial ties and genuine Christian fellowship nonetheless developed. In some cases, for example, Episcopal pastors loaned the use of their parishes for Polish National Catholic worship. A warm friendship grew in the 1920s and 1930s between Bishop Hodur and several Episcopal prelates, most notably Bishop James Darlington of Harrisburg, Pennsylvania. Nonetheless, some Episcopal circles maintained a reserved attitude due to the PNCC's doctrine. For his part, Bishop Hodur believed that a too close link with the Episcopal Church would weaken the PNCC as an institution. When an American prelate suggested that the PNCC should formally affiliate with the Episcopal Church and that Bishop Hodur should become in effect an Episcopal suffragan in charge of Polish affairs, the Polish National Catholic leader refused on the grounds that this would lead to that assimilation which the Poles had resisted in the Roman fold. No doubt largely for these reasons neither the Episcopal nor the Polish National Catholic Churches formally applied the terms of the Bonn Agreement to America. Such a move would not take place before the Second World War.[18]

Extension to Poland

Given the nationalistic nature of Bishop Hodur and his followers, it proved inevitable that they would seek to extend their work to Poland. Even before they sought to do this, however, a native Polish group successfully sought recognition from the Old Catholics. In 1909 Archbishop Gul consecrated an ex-Roman Catholic priest, John Kowalski, as bishop for the Mariavite Church. The Mariavites, originally organized by a mystic, Felicia Kozlowska, began as a religious order which practised extreme devotion to the Virgin Mary and to the Blessed Sacrament. Expelled by Rome and favoured by the Russians, the Mariavites flourished for a time. Bishop Kowalski, however, gradually led them away from Old Catholic principles. Veneration for their foundress evolved into near idolatry; scandals arose over 'mystical marriages' between priests and nuns; and the bishop began to ordain women priests and bishops. These practices led to the expulsion of the Mariavites from the Utrecht Union in 1924. A schism occurred during 1935 led by Bishop Clement Feldman, who sought to reorganize the Mariavites into a denomination that adhered more closely to Old Catholic norms. Though he periodically petitioned for renewed affiliation with the Utrecht Union, the Old Catholics did not respond affirmatively.[19]

Old Catholicism in Poland instead found a firmer footing with the establishment there of the Polish National Catholic Church. Despite the sympathy he initially felt for the Mariavites and the willingness he manifested on a few occasions for greater cooperation, Bishop Hodur believed that the gospel as practised in the PNCC could more fittingly be transplanted to Polish soil. In 1919, therefore, Bishop Hodur dispatched one of his clergymen, Fr. Bronislaus Krupski, to Poland and directed that he investigate the possibilities for the success of such an endeavour. Fr. Krupski largely confined his activities to the distribution of relief donated by Polish National Catholics, but his reports encouraged Bishop Hodur to organize missions in Poland. Church authorities formally authorized the project in 1922, and they sent Fr. Francis Bonczak, who would be consecrated bishop in 1924, to direct the enterprise. These efforts did not go unnoticed at the Vatican. In an audience with a Polish prelate during February 1923, Pope Pius XI singled out the 'National Church' as a dangerous threat to religion in Poland and advised the government to do what it could to hamper the development of such a movement.[20]

Polish officials needed no encouragement from the pope, for in reborn Poland loyalty to the Roman Church and loyalty to the state were inextricably entwined. The Polish foreign ministry, which followed closely a visit to Poland by Bishop Hodur in 1920, decided that activities by the PNCC there ran contrary to Polish interests. Unlike the United States, where the government respected religious freedom, Poland's authorities considered themselves bound by no such strictures. True, the Polish constitution of 1921 formally guaranteed religious freedom, but only members of recognized denominations enjoyed this right. Because Polish Roman Catholics frequently criticized the PNCC as a creation of Jews, Bolsheviks and Freemasons – charges which Polish officials privately admitted were as false as they were fantastic – the government refused to accord it recognition and forbade it to function publicly.[21]

As an unrecognized denomination, the PNCC could not formally construct, own or maintain sacral structures. Worship had to be conducted privately in homes or other buildings officially owned by individuals. These proscriptions worsened following the negotiation of a concordat between Poland and Rome in 1925. If discovered in liturgical garb of the Latin rite, Polish National Catholic priests were liable to arrest, fines and imprisonment for the 'impersonation' of Catholic clergy. Police not infrequently disrupted the burial of Polish National Catholics, and the state refused to recognize baptisms performed in the PNCC; the latter policy created much confusion insofar as the government utilized the services of clergy to register vital statistics. And where legal prosecution ended, private persecution began. On numerous occasions the Catholic Action organization incited acts of physical violence against church members. Petitions to the Polish government for redress did not significantly alter the situation. Nonetheless, a handful of daring clergy managed to organize about twenty-two congregations by December 1927.[22]

Equally deleterious to the establishment of the PNCC in Poland, however, was an ever-present lack of loyal clergy. A shortage of priests plagued the parent church in America. Bishop Hodur therefore found it increasingly necessary to rely upon native Poles, some of whom proved to be motivated more by opportunism than by a sincere attachment to Polish National Catholic principles. This held particularly true of those who sought to evade legal restrictions through affiliation with other recognized denominations. Some priests tried to tie the PNCC to the Orthodox Church, others to various Protestant groups. Bishop Hodur staunchly opposed all such efforts. Moreover, several clergy grew to resent his desire to regulate the affairs of the church in Poland from America. The PNCC's leader hoped to stem these trends through the consecration of Fr. Ladislaus Faron in 1930 as bishop for Poland. The choice proved disastrous, for Bishop Faron reportedly proceeded to preside over marriages of divorced persons; to seek union with Poland's small but legalized Calvinist community; and generally to act in a 'dictatorial' fashion. As a result, Bishop Faron was deposed in 1931, but about one-half of the existing parishes departed with him. The ensuing schism seriously weakened the PNCC in Poland, but Bishop Hodur remained undeterred. He sent Fr. Joseph Padewski to Poland with a mandate to repair the damage. Fr. Padewski, consecrated bishop in 1936, worked hard, and his labours did not go unrequited. On the eve of World War II the mission church numbered approximately fifty-six congregations. Moreover, Bishop Padewski established ties of friendship with his German counterpart, Bishop Erwin Kreuzer of Bonn, whose consecration the Polish priest had attended.[23]

The War Years

By the eve of the Second World War Bishop Padewski had placed the mission church on a sound footing and had won a greater measure of toleration from the government. The German assault on Poland in 1939 changed the situation drastically. The war cut off practically all contact with the parent church in America. As a denomination which cultivated Polish patriotism, the PNCC naturally became the object of much suspicion on the part of the Nazi occupiers. Polish National Catholic parishes in lands directly annexed to the Reich faced liquidation, and their priests often found themselves in labour or concentration camps. Several died at Nazi hands.

The fate of those parishes in the region of Poland organized into the 'General Government' developed differently. Bishop Padewski's contacts with Bishop Kreuzer, as well no doubt as a desire of the Germans to divide the Poles, resulted ironically in the legalization of the church on 22 April 1941. The Nazis, however, denied it use of its original title and instead required that it bear the name 'Old Catholic Church of the Union of Utrecht'. Bishop Padewski, powerless to alter this state of affairs, reconciled himself to the only viable alternative to liquidation. But most church members remained Polish patriots who quietly protested against the German regime. Some of these protests, such as the continued display of national emblems in churches, resulted in threats of punitive action by the Nazis. Moreover, as an American citizen, Bishop Padewski faced increasing interference in ecclesiastical affairs. Arrested in September 1942 and interned in Bavaria, he returned to the United States during March 1944 through the intercession of the American Red Cross. Meanwhile, Fr. Frederick Lachmayr assumed charge of the church in

Poland, and he did what he deemed necessary to preserve the Polish denomination from still further reprisals.[24]

The course of the war nonetheless decimated the ranks of the clergy and brought the PNCC in Poland to the brink of collapse. In September 1944, after it had become more apparent that the Soviet-sponsored 'Lublin Committee' would govern Poland, several Polish National Catholic priests approached the *de facto* authorities and requested legislation. Along with this there surfaced a plan to merge the PNCC with the 'Mariavite Old Catholic Church' and the 'Polish Old Catholic Church'. The former was comprised of those Mariavites who in some measure had returned to Old Catholic practices, and the latter included the few remaining adherents of the deposed Bishop Faron. The plan came to nought, and Polish National Catholic priests renewed their request for recognition by the government in September 1945. The latter accorded this recognition in February 1946.[25]

Though its possibilities for direct action to ease the plight of their co-religionists in Poland were limited, American Polish National Catholics did not remain inactive during the war. Like most Polish Americans, members of the PNCC maintained a lively interest in the land of their ancestors, even though the younger generation increasingly concentrated their attention on events in the United States. Immediately after the outbreak of hostilities the American church organized a campaign to collect and distribute aid to Poland. Avid supporters of wartime policies pursued by the American government, Polish National Catholic officials nonetheless sought membership in the Polish American Congress, an almost exclusively Roman Catholic organization which called for the emergence of a genuinely independent Poland and which protested against the imposition of Soviet hegemony there. Here members of the PNCC would play a small but significant role. They demanded that the Polish American Congress express support for religious freedom in postwar Poland and won their point. Indeed, a Polish official serving in America perhaps best summed up the PNCC's role when he reported in 1940 that Polish National Catholics were 'relatively small in number but active and clamorous . . .' And to this they joined a realistic, if not uncritical, appraisal of postwar political developments in Poland. They endorsed requests for recognition of the mission church by the 'Lublin Committee', and Bishop Padewski returned to Poland to renew his labours.[26]

Subsequent Developments: Poland

Recognition by the increasingly anti-Roman Catholic regime and the return of Bishop Padewski did not, however, ensure either peace or prosperity for the Polish church. True, the denomination could now function openly and even received from the government several churches vacated during the postwar territorial reorganization of the Polish state. Nevertheless, both Bishop Padewski and the links between the Polish and American churches became casualties of the cold war. His American citizenship once again proved a liability, and Bishop Padewski also encountered some opposition from those clergy who strove to gain further autonomy for the church in Poland. In 1951, during the height of Stalinist repression, government authorities arrested the bishop. He died under unclear circumstances in a Warsaw prison on 10 May 1951. His clergy thereupon proceeded to proclaim the 'autocephaly' of the denomination and to rename it the 'Polish Catholic Church'. An administrative overhaul followed, and the church drew up a new code of canon law. A synod in December 1952 elected Fr. Julian Pekala bishop, and he received consecration from two 'Old Catholic Mariavite' bishops and one prelate who had been affiliated with the deposed Bishop Faron. Given the adverse political climate that then obtained, the PNCC in America was unable to exert very much influence on these developments.[27]

Under the leadership of Prime Bishop Leon Grochowski, who succeeded Bishop Hodur upon his demise in 1953, a rapprochement occurred that was in large measure facilitated by the process of de-Stalinization in Poland after 1956. Bishop Pekala resigned his position, and a synod of the Polish Catholic Church elected Fr. Maximilian Rode, an ex-Roman Catholic priest, as his successor. Bishop Grochowski performed the consecration on 5 July 1959 at Utrecht with the assistance of Old Catholic bishops. Following a period of great activity, which included the division of the church into three dioceses (Warsaw, Wroclaw and Cracow), government authorities requested the resignation of Bishop Rode, and Bishop Pekala returned to office in 1965. Nonetheless, despite the fact that by then the Polish Catholic Church had distanced itself considerably from many of Bishop Hodur's ideas, it reaffirmed its spiritual links to the American church.

And these ties grew stronger during the latter 1960s and 1970s as a result of mutual visits and joint projects. The PNCC in America effectively recognized the autonomy of the Polish Catholic Church, and the latter's role changed from that of daughter to that of sister. Not long after Bishop Pekala's return and following another administrative reorganization, Bishop Thaddeus R. Majewski, also consecrated by Bishop Grochowski, assumed office as 'Presiding Bishop'. Under Bishop Majewski's leadership the church has prospered. By the close of 1976 it claimed nearly 29,000 adherents in eighty-four parishes. And though, like other Old Catholic Churches, it has not attained large numerical growth, it enjoys a lively intellectual life. For example, it publishes a scholarly journal *Poslannictwo (The Mission)* along with a popular weekly *Rodzina (The Family)*. The church's positive attitude toward government policies has further ensured the position of the denomination. In 1959 the state authorized establishment of the 'Social Association of Polish Catholics'. Members of the latter manage an industrial organization, 'Polkat', which operates several factories throughout Poland. Revenues derived from this enterprise help fund charitable activities and provide much funding for the Polish Catholic Church.

   In addition to these activities, the Polish Catholic Church has maintained an active participation in the ecumenical movement. A member of the World Council of Churches, the church also belongs to the Polish Ecumenical Council. Both Bishop Rode and Bishop Majewski have emphasized the denomination's affiliation with the Utrecht Union. In fact, for the first time in its history, the International Bishops' Conference met in Poland during 1979. The Polish Catholic Church also has entered into negotiations with the 'Mariavite Old Catholic Church' aimed at the latter's readmission into the Utrecht Union. While such an affiliation has not yet come about, a state of *de facto* intercommunion exists between the two churches. Full participants in Old Catholic dialogue with the Orthodox, the Polish Catholics moreover have given increased attention in recent times to intercommunion with Anglicans. For its part, the English Section of the St. Willibrord Society has facilitated this by supplying books to the Polish Catholic seminary.

Subsequent Developments: America

For the PNCC in America the postwar years marked a gradual dissociation from intense Polish national feeling and from the use of the Polish language. The complexion of the church membership had changed. Many younger Polish Americans no longer spoke the language of their forefathers; moreover, as the former rose on the social scale they felt a greater affinity with American society at large. Under the leadership of Bishop Grochowski, the PNCC continued to emphasize its mission among Polish Americans but also recognized the need for accommodation to these changed conditions. In short, what the church now had to do was to seek a new balance between considerations of ethnicity on the one hand and those of Catholicity on the other. This manifested itself above all through the introduction of English as a liturgical language along with Polish. Though the matter underwent study during the 1940s, formal approval of an English mass occurred at a General Synod in 1958.[28]

Another important response to these conditions was a greater participation in the ecumenical movement and, above all, the formal adoption of intercommunion with the Episcopal Church on the basis of the Bonn Agreement. The PNCC joined both the World Council of Churches and the National Council of Churches in the United States. Support for the extension of the Bonn Agreement to America gained ground in the late 1930s and early 1940s. The Episcopal Church approved intercommunion with the Utrecht Union in 1934 and 1940. In 1943 Episcopal officials attempted to secure official approval of intercommunion by the PNCC, but the latter, perhaps because of reservations voiced earlier by Bishop Hodur, did not act until 1946, when a General Synod ratified the Bonn accord.[29] Apart from ecumenical considerations and a desire to conform to the relationship as it had developed in Europe, Polish National Catholic leaders also regarded intercommunion as a provisional solution to a pastoral problem: under the new agreement PNCC members who travelled or relocated to areas far away from a parish of their own could now receive the sacraments in an Episcopal church. This constituted the most visible fruit of intercommunion, as well as the periodic participation by bishops of the respective churches in each other's episcopal consecrations. To follow up these developments, a joint Intercommunion Commission was appointed to discuss the specific application of the Bonn accord in America. Moreover, the PNCC and the Anglican Church of Canada officially established intercommunion in 1958.

During Bishop Grochowski's tenure the PNCC attained the peak of its growth, for in 1962 it claimed approximately 160 parishes with a membership of well over 100,000. The use of English as a liturgical language increased after his successor, Prime Bishop Thaddeus F. Zielinski, assumed office in 1969. In 1967 the PNCC established a diocese in Canada based at Toronto. The quadrennial General Synod, as the church's highest administrative body, assumed a greater role in the determination of ecclesiastical policy. In addition, Bishop Zielinski strengthened relations with the European Old Catholics and the 1977 session of the International Bishops' Conference convened in Scranton.

Along with this there surfaced a desire to extend the work of the church among people not of Polish background. Some members even called for the elimination of the word 'Polish' from the denomination's title. This emerged directly out of a growing realization that changes within the Roman Church, such as the adoption of the vernacular, tended to reduce the PNCC's appeal to most Polish Americans. Under Bishop Zielinski's leadership the PNCC effectively reduced its ethnic identification and instead represented itself more as a democratic yet traditional form of Catholicism in America. In fact, a rather paradoxical neoconservatism, based upon a respectful de-emphasis of Bishop Hodur's ideas and supported by many of the younger clergy, began to emerge by the later 1970s. For instance, the liturgical reforms promoted by Bishop Zielinski, including the celebration of mass facing the congregation, nonetheless preserved the Tridentine rite virtually intact.

This neoconservatism has set the PNCC apart from those American churches which have engaged in experimentation and innovation in the areas of theology, liturgy, and discipline. Moreover, it has played no small role in the termination of intercommunion in North America. After the 1950s both Episcopalians and Polish National Catholics permitted the Intercommunion Commission to become dormant. The ordination of women by the Episcopal Church, adopted in 1976, posed a particular threat to intercommunion, given the fact that the International Bishops' Conference had expressed opposition to such a practice. In 1977 Bishop Zielinski, who had enjoyed a warm friendship with several Episcopal prelates, suspended intercommunion with both Episcopalians and Canadian Anglicans, as the latter also had adopted women's ordination. At the root of the issue was whether the PNCC could maintain a sacramental relationship with churches some of whose clergy it could not recognize as validly ordained. A General Synod in 1978 supplied the answer when it voted to terminate intercommunion in North America.[30]

The 1978 General Synod also elected Bishop Francis C. Rowinski to succeed Bishop Zielinski, who retired at that time after a lengthy career of service. Like his European brother bishops, Prime Bishop Rowinski leads a church confronted by a growing tide of secularism. Secure in America, the PNCC has entered into the development of several programmes designed to strengthen it further in the fields of Christian education, scholarship, mission, and administration. Today the PNCC numbers 153 congregations in five North American dioceses. The Polish National Union, its affiliated fraternal insurance organization, has prospered as well. The Union contributes towards the maintenance of the church's Savonarola Theological Seminary at Scranton and operates a large residence for the elderly. Moreover, the PNCC remains committed to the ecumenical movement. Dialogue has begun with the Orthodox, and cordial contacts with Episcopalians continue. Indeed, Bishop Rowinski clearly demonstrated the importance attached to relations with Anglicans when he attended celebrations in commemoration of the Bonn Agreement at London during July 1981.[31]

What does the future hold in store for the Polish National Catholic and the Polish Catholic Churches? Clearly, the PNCC will attempt to preserve in some measure its Polish ethnic heritage, but it will do so with the understanding that it is primarily an American institution. Its attachment to Old Catholicism has ensured that even the election of a Polish pontiff, John Paul II, will not cause it to doubt the need for its existence. As the only American member of the Union of Utrecht, it will seek to cooperate closely with its European sister churches but will develop missionary strategies appropriate to conditions in the United States and Canada. Relations with the Anglican Communion will remain cordial. The future of the Polish Catholic Church appears less certain, given the recent economic and political developments in Poland. Nonetheless, the Polish church has overcome serious obstacles in the past, and there is no reason to doubt that it will do so in the future as well.

NOTES

1. Laurence Orzell, 'A Minority within a Minority: The Polish National Catholic Church, 1896–1907', *Polish American Studies*, xxxvi (Spring 1979), pp. 5–32.

2. John Iwicki, *The First One Hundred Years: A Study of the Apostolate of the Congregation of the Resurrection in the United States, 1866–1966* (Rome, 1966), pp. 79–88.

3. Ibid., pp. 94–5.

4. Laurence J. Orzell, 'The "National Catholic" Response: Franciszek Hodur and His Followers, 1897–1907', unpublished paper presented at St. Michael's College, University of Toronto, 25 Oct. 1980.

5. Gen. Alexander Kirejew, 'Der Altkatholizismus und die Polnische Frage', *Révue Internationale de Théologie*, vii (1899), pp. 12–18.

6. Wenceslaus Kruszka, *Historya Polska w Ameryce* (Milwaukee, 1905), II, pp. 49–50. Archbishop Vilatte, allegedly consecrated by Jacobites in Ceylon during 1892, ordained as a bishop Fr. Stephen Kaminski, an 'Independent' leader at Buffalo, New York, in 1898. Following the latter's demise in 1911 his followers joined the Polish National Catholic Church.

7. Kozlowski to Grafton, 3 April 1901, Kozlowski File, Grafton Papers, Grafton House, Fond du Lac. See also Charles C. Grafton, *A Journey Godward* (Milwaukee, 1910), pp. 279–87.

8. Grafton, *A Journey Godward*, pp. 288–94.

9. *New York Times*, 26 Feb. 1903, p. 5.

10. *De Oud-Katholiek*, Mar. 1907, pp. 31–2.

11. The material for the section 'A Surer Foundation' has been drawn from the author's essay 'The "National Catholic" Response', cited above, and from his 'Franciszek Hodur and the Old Catholics, 1899–1908', *PNCC Studies*, i (1980), pp. 13–23.

12. Laurence J. Orzell, 'The Polish National Catholic Church: Past and Present', unpublished paper presented at St. Mary's College, Orchard Lake, Michigan, 25 June 1981.

13. An English translation of *Our Faith* has been published under the title *Our Way of Life* (Scranton, n.d.), no pagination. See also *The Confession of Faith and Eleven Great Principles* (Scranton, 1978), pp. 4–7.

14. *Our Way of Life*, n.p.; *The Confession of Faith*, pp. 33–6.

15. *Our Way of Life*, n.p.

16. 'Protokoll der Bischofskonferenz in Köln', 11 Sept. 1913, Archives of the Archbishops of Utrecht, Utrecht. Hereafter abbreviated *AAU*.

17. Kenninck to Hodur, 16 June 1928; same to same, 24 Sept. 1931; both in File 'Hodur, Fr. II', *AAU*. See also *Rola Boza*, 8 Aug. 1931, p. 254.

18. Anthony Müller, Canon of All Saints Episcopal Cathedral, Milwaukee, to Bishop Erwin Kreuzer, Bonn, 13 May 1936, File 'Hodur, Fr. II', *AAU*. See also *Rola Boza*, 10 May 1930, p. 156.

19. For a valuable study of Mariavitism, see Jerry Peterkiewicz, *The Third Adam* (London, 1975).

20. General Department, Polish Ministry of Foreign Affairs, to Ministry of Religious Affairs and Public Education, 27 Mar. 1923, File 1381, *Archiwum Akt Nowych* (Archives of Contemporary Documents), Warsaw. Hereafter cited *AAN*.

21. Same to same, 20 Sept. 1920, File 1381, *AAN*. See also Stephen Wlodarski, *Historia Kościoła Polskokatolickiego* (Warsaw, 1964), *passim*.

22. Wlodarski, *Historia*, pp. 145–58.

23. Ibid., pp. 281–304.

24. *Verordnungsblatt für das Generalgouvernement*, 28 Apr. 1941, pp. 213–14; General Affairs Division, General Government, to Padewski, 28 June 1941, copy supplied to author by Fr. Victor Wysoczanski, Professor at the Christian Theological Academy, Warsaw. See also Fr. Wysoczanski's *Polski Nurt Starokatolicyzmu* (Warsaw, 1977), pp. 107–8.

25. Wysoczanski, *Polski Nurt Starokatolicyzmu*, pp. 108–12.

26. Charles Ripa to Polish Embassy at Washington, 21 Mar. 1940, Records of the Ministry of Foreign Affairs, File 174, *AAN*.

27. The material for the section 'Subsequent Developments: Poland' has been drawn largely from Wysoczanski, *Polski Nurt Starokatolicyzmu*, pp. 113–38.

28. Unless otherwise noted, the developments discussed in the section 'Subsequent Developments: America' have been derived from the author's paper 'The Polish National Catholic Church: Past and Present', cited above.

29. The Right Revd. Frank E. Wilson, 'Memorandum on the Polish National Catholic Church', 18 June 1943, Records of the Advisory Council to the Presiding Bishop on Ecclesiastical Relations, Episcopal Church Centre, New York.

30. The minutes of the 1978 General Synod have been published under the title *Fifteenth General Synod of the Polish National Catholic Church* (Scranton, 1979). See especially pp. 176–219 and Appendix II.

31. The PNCC adopted a programme of missionary work among Poles in Brazil during the 1970s, but this effort has virtually collapsed due to Roman Catholic opposition and a lack of competent clerical leadership.

5

The Society of St. Willibrord

(a) Its History

JOHN BURLEY

It was a dramatic and moving moment as the whole Convocation of Canterbury rose and recited the Doxology, for on that day, 22 January 1932, the Church of England entered into full communion with the Old Catholic Churches, the Lower House of Canterbury having just concurred with the decision of the Upper House taken two days earlier to establish intercommunion between the Church of England and the Old Catholic Churches. On 21 January 1932 both Houses of the Convocation of York had passed the same resolution. *The York Journal of Convocation* ends its report of the debate on the resolution with the words: ' . . . and it was passed unanimously amid applause'.

Thus the chief aim of the Society of St. Willibrord, founded in 1908, was at last realized – that end for which it had prayed and worked for almost a quarter of a century. The Society was founded exactly fifty years after the publication of John Mason Neale's famous work *A History of the So-called Jansenist Church of Holland* had brought the Old Catholics to the attention of English churchmen. Neale's book created a new interest in the Old Catholic Church and during the fifty years following its publication there were many personal contacts between Anglicans and Old Catholics.

The Lambeth Conference Report of 1908 records that 'The Conference desires to maintain and strengthen the friendly relations which already exist between the Churches of the Anglican Communion and the ancient Church of Holland and the Old Catholic Churches, especially in Germany, Switzerland and Austria.' It was within the context of such official encouragement that the need was felt for an unofficial association which would work and pray for closer relations between the Anglican and Old Catholic Churches. In 1908 letters on the subject began to appear in *The Guardian* – a church newspaper now defunct – and on 28 October of that year it published the following notice:

THE SOCIETY OF ST. WILLIBRORD

The Society of St. Willibrord, which is now in process of formation, is intended to be a medium by which closer intercommunion between the Old Catholics and the Church of England may be brought about. The Archbishop of Utrecht is Patron. The Bishop of Gibraltar will be the first Anglican President, while Monseigneur J. J. van Thiel, D.D., will act in a similar capacity on the Old Catholic side.[1]

There followed a list of Anglican and Old Catholic Vice-Presidents, and a note that the Revds. G. E. Barber and D. Bridge would be General Secretaries of the new society, and that its committee would consist of twelve clerical and twelve lay members. According to the Minute Book, the first formal committee was held on 7 January 1909, but there had been previous meetings of which, unfortunately, we have no record.

When the committee of the SSW published the Lambeth Conference Resolutions, it added a note on the actual state of relations between the two Churches as it was in 1908: 'These may be reasonably termed a state of individual intercommunion'. The committee confidently ended its statement: 'Mutual intercourse and, above all, a full use of those privileges of individual intercommunion which already exist will undoubtedly, in God's good time, bring about a complete mutual understanding between Anglicans and Old Catholics, and a Union between them which shall tend to the greater Glory of God, and to the final re-union of the whole of Christ's Holy Catholic Church.'

This, then, was the task to which the newly formed society now addressed itself, a task that occupied it for nearly a quarter of a century before its aim was realized.

An early (undated) leaflet records the Objects and Rules of the Society:

OBJECT: To promote friendly relations between the Anglican and Old Catholic Churches, and to prepare the way for the restoration of full intercommunion between them, especially by the following methods:-
(1) By publishing accurate information as to the historical, theological and practical standpoints of both communions.
(2) By conveying information about the Old Catholic Churches to all Anglican chaplains residing in Old Catholic centres.

(3) By welcoming and entertaining Old Catholics visiting England and other English-speaking countries and vice-versa.

There follow nine Rules concerning membership, Officers, etc. and ending with a commitment to use the 'Prayer of the Society' which is the Collect for Unity.

During the first five years, the committee of the SSW included some distinguished names. Among them were the Revd. Dr. G. C. Richards, Canon T. A. Lacey and Father F. W. Puller, SSJE, Dr. Percy Dearmer, Dr. W. J. Sparrow-Simpson and the President, Bishop W. E. Collins of Gibraltar. Unfortunately, Bishop Collins died in 1911. He was succeeded as President by the Bishop of Willesden, the Right Revd. W. W. Perrin.

The second committee meeting was held on 1 June 1909. It considered a memorandum on the constitutional position of Bishop Mathew, who had chaired the first meeting. The activities of Bishop Mathew were to occupy the committee until 1913, when it 'noted with thankfulness' the formal ex-communication of Arnold Harris Mathew by all the Old Catholic bishops sitting in the Bishops' Conference at Cologne in September of that year. As Dr. Gordon Huelin remarked in his excellent little book on *St. Willibrord and his Society*: 'we may almost hear the sighs of relief on the part of its members'.[2] Bishop Mathew had caused not only much embarrassment to the newly formed SSW, but also considerable mischief both in the Old Catholic Church and the Church of England.[3]

Fortunately, this second committee was also concerned with more positive and fruitful matters. It set up a Literature Committee to consider suitable publications and decided that priests in sympathy with the aims of the Society should be invited to celebrate the Eucharist on behalf of the Society on St. Willibrord's day, 7 November. This practice, begun in 1909, has continued to the present day.

The year 1913, which saw the fifth birthday of the Society, was marked with enthusiasm, hard work and careful planning on the part of the officers and committee, with the help of many friends of the Society. With the Bishop of Willesden in the chair, the committe met five times. In September, the ninth Old Catholic Congress was held in Cologne. The Bishop of Willesden represented the Church of England, bringing greetings from the Archbishop of Canterbury. The Revd. G. E. Barber was the official representative of the SSW. Dr. Huelin comments: 'An English visitor attending the Congress remarked that he noted a distinct increase of friendship towards the Anglican Church, shown in several ways, and he came away both hopeful and encouraged.'[4]

Early in November Bishop Prins of Haarlem, a Vice-President of the Society, arrived in England. The Archbishop of Canterbury invited him to lunch at Lambeth and he spent three days with Bishop Gore during a visit to Oxford. Then back to London for the great day Friday 7 November 1913, the Feast of St. Willibrord, at St Mary's, Charing Cross Road, where the Bishop of Willesden, as Anglican President, sang the Solemn Eucharist, assisted by the secretary, the Revd. G. E. Barber. That evening, at the public meeting held in Church House, Westminster, Bishop Prins conveyed greetings from the Old Catholic Church in Holland and especially from the Archbishop of Utrecht and the Bishop of Deventer, the newly appointed Old Catholic President of the Society.

The following Sunday evening the final service of the Festival was held at St. James's Church, Hampstead, where Fr. Barber was assistant priest. 'The climax came to a momentous week when the Bishop of Haarlem, with his brother bishops of Willesden and Northern and Central Europe bedside him, turned, and with deep emotion pronounced the Blessing.' In his book *St. Willibrord and his Society*, under the chapter so aptly headed 'Years of Perseverance', Dr. Huelin continues: 'This was the first time that a bishop of the Church of Holland had paid an official visit to England – and it marked the crowning achievement of all the efforts made by the Society of St. Willibrord during the early years of this century to encourage deeper understanding with the Old Catholics.'[5]

This Festival in November 1913 marked the end of the first phase of the Society's mission, which came to an abrupt halt with the outbreak of World War 1 in August 1914 and, in the same month, the death of its founder and first secretary, George Barber. In view of the satisfactory 'growing together' of Anglicans and Old Catholics, especially the Dutch, in this pre-war period, culminating in 1913 with the successful official visit and Festival, one would have expected to see an immediate revival of the Society in the post-war period and a rapid extension of its work. Inexplicably, whilst the war ended after four years, the Society remained moribund for fourteen! After the passing of more than fifty years, the time has come to recall some unrecorded history.[6]

It was entirely due to the persistence and tact of the redoubtable

Canon J. A. Douglas that the Society was revived at all. By this time (1928), most of the original committee had died. The Bishop of Willesden was still technically President but, although he had made no effort to revive the Society, yet he refused to part with the Minutes and other records. It was an awkward situation. Quietly and calmly, Canon Douglas cut the Gordian knot by going straight to Archbishop Randall Davidson with the problem. Archbishop Davidson also saw the importance of reviving the Society, so that when 'J.A.D.' proposed as a solution, that he himself be entrusted with the task of getting the Society on its feet again, he gladly charged him with that duty.

It is a measure of Canon Douglas's skill that the first meeting of the re-constituted Society on the 20 March 1928 was both convened and chaired by the President. The Bishop of Willesden proposed that those present should act as an executive committee for the purpose of (1) reconstituting the Society; (2) carrying on liason work and such other work as might be desirable until the Society should be re-established. Canon Douglas proposed the Revd. C. B. Moss and Mr. W. R. V. Brade as Secretaries and they were asked (1) to revise the role of members (2) to revise the Rules (3) to report to a meeting of the Society to be held not later than the autumn. Mr. Moss wrote the Minutes and tactfully headed them: 'The Society of St. Willibrord, after having been in abeyance for fourteen years, was revived by the President, the Bishop of Willesden, in 1928.'

The Minutes of the following meeting significantly record that: 'A meeting of the committee was held on 6 July 1928 in consequence of the resignation of the Bishop of Willesden from the office of President, owing to his age.' At the next meeting on 29 October 1928, the Bishop of Fulham, Dr. Staunton Batty, was welcomed as the new President, the archives of the Society were duly handed over to Canon Douglas as Librarian and the subscription fixed at 2/6d. (12½p.).

The acceptance of Anglican Orders by the Oecumenical Patriarchate in 1922 changed the whole climate of Anglican/Old Catholic relations. Canon Douglas had already been in touch with Archbishop Kenninck of Utrecht on the subject of Orders, but the Dutch had remained doubtful. Now the time was right for a positive step forward and Archbishop Kenninck appointed a fresh commission for an objective study of Anglican ordinations. The Commission reported favourably and on 2 June 1925 the Archbishop of Utrecht wrote to the Archbishop of Canterbury that the Church of Utrecht formally accepted Anglican Orders as valid. Thus the last great barrier between the two Churches was removed. Accordingly, an official delegation from the Old Catholic Churches came to the Lambeth Conference in 1930.

This was the first time that an Archbishop of Utrecht had visited England and the first time that an official delegation from the Old Catholic Churches had come specifically *to discuss the possibilities of reunion*. Their first discussion with a committee of the Lambeth Conference took place on 16 July 1930 with Dr. Headlam, Bishop of Gloucester, in the chair. Three days later a second meeting was held, when four more Anglican Bishops were brought in, together with three advisers – Canon J. A. Douglas, Dr. C. B. Moss and the Revd. Dr. W. Chauncey Emhardt of the American Episcopal Church. On both occasions there were long and searching discussions in which a wide measure of agreement was reached.[7]

In the years between the wars Canon Douglas and Dr Moss were to make a notable contribution to the work of the Society. Dr. Moss emerges as an authority on the Old Catholic Churches, gradually gaining the respect and trust of the Old Catholic bishops, who could understand his exposition of the Anglican position and of the different schools of thought within the Church of England. Already, in 1927, Moss had written a small book on *The Old Catholic Churches and Reunion* for the benefit of Anglicans. Now, for the benefit of the Old Catholic laity, who knew little about Anglicanism, he wrote a long pamphlet called *The Anglican Churches* which was translated into Dutch and German.

The Report of the Lambeth Conference brought the question of reunion with Old Catholics clearly before Anglicans. The following year the Archbishop of Canterbury appointed a commission to enter into formal negotiations with a similar commission representing the Old Catholic Churches. C. B. Moss was appointed joint-secretary with the Revd. C. L. Gage-Brown, who acted as interpreter, and Professor Andreas Rinkel (later Archbishop of Utrecht) as secretary of the Old Catholic commission. This joint conference, which elected the Bishop of Gloucester as Chairman, met on 2 July 1931 at Bonn. Complete agreement was reached in one day.[8] It is significant to note that, apart from Dr. Headlam, all the Anglicans were members of the Society of St. Willibrord.

The Bonn Agreement was promptly ratified by the Episcopal

Synod of the Old Catholic Churches meeting in Vienna on 7 September 1931 and by the Convocations of Canterbury and York on 21/22 January 1932. It must be remembered that this Agreement, in the first instance, was only with the Church of England. Nevertheless, despite the upheavals of war, the whole Anglican Communion had affirmed it within twenty years. Thus, the Old Catholic Churches are in 'full communion' with all Anglican Churches. Although the term 'inter-communion' was used in the original Statement, it is now always referred to as 'Full communion', the Lambeth Conference of 1958 (Resolution 14) having recommended that unrestricted mutual recognition, including acceptance of ministries, should be called 'Full communion'.

How does it work out in practice? It means that every Anglican Communicant is entitled to receive Communion in Old Catholic Churches and vice versa. Bishops, both Anglican and Old Catholic, periodically take part in one another's consecrations, described by 'J. A. D.' as 'the mingling of the streams'.[9] In the autumn of that year, the Bishop of Deventer, Mgr. J. H. Berends, with eight Old Catholic priests, came to England, where the SSW arranged their itinerary. They attended a Sung Eucharist at St Paul's Cathedral, where they all received Holy Communion. The Annual Meeting of the Society was arranged to coincide with this visit and the address of welcome was given by the new Bishop of Kensington, Dr. B. F. Simpson, who reminded his audience that, together with the Bishop in Jerusalem, he was 'the offspring of the two churches'.

With its main objective achieved, it was perhaps inevitable that the Society should find itself somewhat lost: there were even those who thought it should be disbanded. Time was required to assess the effect of the Bonn Agreement upon the two churches and to discover new needs to serve: there is little of interest to report on during the post-war period until, in 1938, a letter was received by Canon Douglas from the Old Catholic Section of the Society. The seventh of November, 1939, would be the twelfth centenary of the death of St. Willibrord. Special services were being arranged at Utrecht, together with an exhibition. The letter expressed the hope that the Archbishop of Canterbury would be able to arrange similar celebrations in England.

At a meeting of the committee on 14 February 1939, it was arranged that the Bishop of Fulham, the Dean of Chichester and the Hon. Secretary (Dr. Moss) should go to Holland for this occasion. It was also suggested that the Archbishop of Utrecht might be invited to preach at Westminster Abbey. The Minutes of the last pre-war meeting in July 1939 record: 'a Service in Commemoration of St. Willibrord was to be held in Westminster Abbey on 19 November, at which the Archbishop of Canterbury would celebrate'. World War II prevented the fulfilment of this plan, but the visit of the Anglican members to Holland did take place – the last real contact for several years. Dr. Huelin recalls:

After a hazardous and difficult journey, the official Anglican Delegation, consisting of the Bishops of Gloucester and Fulham, Canon Douglas and the Revd. P. Usher, arrived at Utrecht on the eve of St. Willibrord's Day and, in view of the circumstances in which they had made the journey, they were given a singularly warm welcome by the Dutch authorities.[10]

Although World War II had begun, this journey was still possible in November 1939, but on 10 May 1940, Holland was invaded and the little Dutch forces overwhelmed near Arnhem. Opposite the military cemetery stands their memorial: 'Freedom lost' and, five years later, 'Freedom restored'.

At this point all communications with the continent ceased and the work of the Society came to an abrupt halt: how nearly it ceased altogether is recorded in the Minutes of the last two meetings already mentioned. Had it done so, there would have been no means of reconvening immediately after the war, nor of making the important contributions to mutual understanding and friendship which Mr. Jack Witten describes elsewhere.

It has already been pointed out that, following upon the Bonn Agreement, there were those who felt that the work of the Society had ended. The Minutes of the meeting of 19 February 1939 record that Dr. Moss 'read a memorandum in which he suggested that now that the first object of the Society had been accomplished, the work that remained to be done would be more effectively done by the Council on Foreign Relations of the Church of England than by a small private society'. After considerable discussion, the following resolution was moved by the Dean of Chichester, Dr. A. S. Duncan-Jones, and carried unanimously:

That, subject to the consent of the members of the Anglican Section of the Society, the work of the Society should be handed over to the Council on Foreign Relations: assurance being given by the C. F. R. that steps shall be taken to continue the promotion of mutual knowledge and friendship between the Church of England and the Old Catholic Churches.

However, Canon J. A. Douglas was absent from this meeting and its members had not reckoned on his reaction: the Minutes of the next and final pre-war meeting on 19 July record bleakly that: 'The Resolution passed at the last committee meeting to hand over the work of the Society to the Council on Foreign Relations was rescinded, because Canon Douglas, as Secretary of the C.F.R., opposed the scheme so strongly that it was clearly impracticable.' So a crisis was averted and the Society remained in nominal existence for five weary years, awaiting the day of 'Freedom Restored'.

As World War II drew to its close, this time the SSW was ready and waiting to go into action. About a fortnight before the end of the war in Europe the Committee met to plan for the future. A sub-committee was appointed 'to prepare a revised Constitution for submission to a general meeting.' A fortnight after V.E. Day the committee re-assembled and Canon Douglas's revision of the Constitution was passed for recommendation to the general meeting to be called on 24 July 1945. Dr. Moss was asked to write to the Archbishop of Utrecht (Dr. Rinkel) inviting him to England for consultation. Meanwhile the Bishop of Fulham (Dr. Staunton Batty) had already written to the Church papers asking that part of the money raised by the Churches for 'Christian Reconstruction in Europe' (CRE) should be allocated for the benefit of the Old Catholic Churches and suggesting that particular parishes might sponsor particular Old Catholic parishes.

In July about thirty people assembled at Westminster for the General Meeting, where the new constitution – already circulated to members – was adopted with certain amendments. Two leading members of the old Committee had died – Mr. W. R. V. Brade, Lay Secretary, and the Revd. Dr. N. P. Williams, Lady Margaret Professor of Divinity at Oxford. To strengthen the existing committee new members were elected, including the Revd. E. W. Kemp (later to become Theological Secretary and now Bishop of Chichester), and J. B. Dakin (one of the Directors of CRE). Mr. Dakin and Mr. Kemp undertook to assist Dr. Moss with the secretarial duties.

Thus strengthened, the Society began its post-war activities. With the establishment of inter-communion in 1932, the object of the Society had already been redrafted: 'To promote friendly relations between the Anglican Communion and the Old Catholic Churches, including the fullest use of the inter-communion now established between them'. In order to promote knowledge about the Old

Catholics and the work of the Society, it was decided in 1946 to publish *The St. Willibrord Chronicle*, edited by J. B. Dakin, but, owing to lack of funds, only four numbers were published.

In July 1947 the Archbishop of Utrecht visited London and was received by the Archbishop of Canterbury at a session of the Church Assembly. Afterwards there was a Reception by the Nikaean Club for which Canon Douglas sent out invitations to 'a lunch of Apostolic frugality' (these were still days of rationing). At this Reception the Archbishop of Utrecht received the Lambeth Cross. During this visit, Archbishop Rinkel addressed a meeting of the Society on the past, present and future of the Old Catholic Church.

Next year he returned to England for the opening ceremonies of the Lambeth Conference, which began with a great Service of Reception at Canterbury Cathedral, where the Archbishop of Canterbury welcomed the delegates and observers. A few weeks later, on 17 August 1948, the first post-war International Old Catholic Congress assembled at Hilversum. The Archbishop of Canterbury had asked an American bishop of Dutch origin to be his representative – Dr. Sturtevant, Bishop of Fond du Lac, to whom I was appointed Chaplain. The theme of the Congress was 'The ecumenical movement' in preparation for 'Amsterdam 1948' which followed.

Normally a layman is chosen to be President of these Congresses, but on this occasion the Revd. Professor B. A. van Kleef (father of the present Bishop of Haarlem) was appointed. This was a wise choice, for he proved to be a brilliant President, skilfully guiding the Congress through some difficult months. The grand finale of the Congress was the Rally at the Gooiland Theatre, attended by some six hundred people. Here the Bishop of Fond du Lac, in conveying greetings from the Archbishop of Canterbury and the Presiding Bishop of the Episcopal Church in America, said that our two Communions stood together for Catholic Faith and Order combined with evangelical zeal and Protestant freedom. The Bishop of Edinburgh, Dr. Warner – in whose consecration in 1947 the fourteenth Bishop of Haarlem, J. van der Oord, had taken part – brought greetings from the Scottish Episcopal Church. There followed speeches from the visiting Old Catholic bishops, including one from Bishop Steinwachs who with some unwisdom spoke of the terrible conditions in Germany following the allied bombing – 'only nine Old Catholic churches remain undamaged in the Western Zone'. However true, this was hardly the place to say it, with Rotterdam razed to the ground, including the precious 'hidden' church. With great firmness and tact the President intervened to say that they in Holland also knew what it was to endure the ravages of war: they, too, had not forgotten what they had suffered at the hands of Germans – cities and churches destroyed, people tortured and killed ... 'Yet we can receive you as a friend and brother in the Faith'. The greetings and messages brought by our bishops, especially the Lambeth Resolution on Inter-communion, were hailed with acclamation by the Old Catholics. Their sincere happiness at having us with them was expressed in the warmth of their welcome and the generous hospitality with which we were received into the homes – and hearts – of our Old Catholic hosts. My wife and I were the guests of the Glazemaker family at their delightful farm house. Their son, Antonius, was a server at the Old Catholic church in Hilversum. The last time we met him was at the Jubilee Celebrations of the Bonn Agreement in Utrecht on St. Willibrord Day 1981. This time we were able to greet him as the new Bishop of Deventer!

Meanwhile, the Society of St. Willibrord had been left in a state of suspended animation, due to the sudden departure abroad of Mr. Dakin the Committee had not met since 1946. Accordingly, Herbert Waddams and 'J. A. D.' invited me to meet the President of the Society, Dr. Staunton Batty, former bishop of Fulham, and the secretary, Dr. C. B. Moss. I was asked whether I would take on the secretaryship of the Society. I agreed and was invited to a meeting of the Committee of Lambeth Palace on 27 September 1950. By this time it comprised the Chairman, Canon J. A. Douglas, the secretary, Dr. C. B. Moss, the Revd. E. W. Kemp, Canon F. Hood and Bishop Batty. Present by invitation were the new Bishop of Fulham, the Rt. Revd. George Ingle, the Revd. F. de Jonge, Dr. G. Huelin and the Revd. H. M. Waddams, all of whom I knew. Before proceeding to business, Canon Douglas asked leave to summarize the history of the Society 'If only for the benefit of the future student'. He then read a very interesting paper in the course of which he paid tribute to Dr. C. B. Moss. The business was quickly completed. Those present by invitation were co-opted to the committee. New Officers were elected: Canon Douglas and Dr. Moss were made Vice-Presidents. A meeting was called which took place on 15 November 1950 with the Revd. C. L. Gage-Brown in the Chair. The most important thing that happened at this was the election of Mr. C. J. Witten as Youth Secretary. In welcoming him, the new Secretary said that with his help he hoped the Society would arrange an Anglican-Old Catholic Youth Conference for the summer of 1951 and also a holiday tour in Switzerland. Dr. Gordon Huelin writes: 'A new era began for the Society in 1950 when Dr. J. W. C. Wand, as Bishop of London, accepted the office of President and the Revd. J. Anderson Burley became Honorary Secretary, with Mr. C. J. Witten as the first Youth Secretary. This latter aspect of the Society's work, which has come to the forefront in post-war years, has opened up many new horizons.'[11]

The first youth conference at Brighton in 1951, which was a resounding success, began a new chapter in Anglican/Old Catholic relations and its impact was not soon forgotten. Twenty-three years later, I was representing the SSW at the Old Catholic Congress at Lucerne in 1974, when a middle-aged couple, accompanied by their teen-age children, came up to me, and the father said: 'I don't suppose you remember us, but we were at the first Youth Conference, and we have never forgotten how your wife welcomed the delegates in four languages.'

Over the years, these triennial conferences and annual exchange visits have made a notable contribution towards realizing the object of the Society: 'to promote friendly relations' between Anglicans and Old Catholics, especially among young people who are 'the Church of Tomorrow' – indeed they are already 'the Church of Today'. We owe an inexpressible debt of gratitude to Mr. Jack Witten, until his death Chairman of the Executive Committee of the SSW, for his pioneer work for youth, which not only brought the Society to life again, but made 'inter-communion' a reality for hundreds of young people in both Communions, and for the not-so-young.

A weakness of the SSW from the beginning has been in the field of 'propaganda', about which Canon Douglas frequently complained, but could do little to remedy. Jack Witten's work over the years did something positive to remedy this, not so much in 'publicity' as in personal relations. Widespread ignorance, however, still remains. The time has come to find someone experienced to serve as Public Relations Officer.

Apart from arranging clergy visits, exchange visits at parish level and youth conferences, one of the most important contributions made by the Society has been the periodic conferences between Anglican and Old Catholic theologians. Their value was seen when they were taken over officially by the Council on Foreign Relations.

Looking back over my twenty-five years as secretary and the time since, I had already begun to question whether we had yet, in fact, achieved 'Full Communion', when the Bishop of Chichester's Jubilee lecture reinforced my misgivings. He pointed out that 'a sacramental relationship carries certain implications which go much beyond that of simply receiving Holy Communion together . . . It must imply a community of life, an exchange and a commitment to one another in respect of major decisions on questions of faith and morals.'

It is surely anomalous that Old Catholic bishops should be invited to Lambeth Conferences as 'Observers' in exactly the same category as, for example, Lutherans. Since the Church of England – in 'full communion' with all other Anglican Churches – shares the same relationship with all the Old Catholic Churches, it would seem consistent that the Old Catholic bishops should be invited to the Lambeth Conference as 'Members': but the Lambeth Conference is an assembly of Anglican bishops and the insuperable difficulty appears to be that Old Catholics are not Anglicans! Therefore, the suggestion I would venture to make – as an interim measure, pending a decision by the Lambeth Conference itself – is that Bishops of 'Churches in full Communion' be invited to the *next* Lambeth Conference not simply as 'Observers' but as 'Consultants'. This would at least be one practical step towards rectifying what the Bishop of Chichester, in his lecture, described as the 'failure to provide adequate and regular official organs of consultation, the failure to share sufficiently in theological discussion.' There is undoubtedly need for closer consultation on inter-church relations and matters of principle, such as Ministry and Authority: for true union will come only through a slow and gradual growing together into one hierarchical Communion whose bishops share responsibility for one and all.

So, it seems to me that the work of the Society of St. Willibrord is by no means finished. Just as it made an important contribution towards achieving intercommunion – finally realized in the Bonn Agreement and subsequently built up by mutual knowledge and fellowship during exchange visits and conferences – so, now, following the year of the Golden Jubilee, the SSW faces a further important task in promoting and forwarding *the fullness* of 'Full Communion'. As the Society faces this future, it may find both a warning and an encouragement in recalling the advice of the famous Dr. Jowett of Balliol to a young Cosmo Gordon Lang:

'Don't expect too much and don't attempt too little.'

(b) Youth and other Activities

JACK WITTEN*

A few years after the Bonn Agreement of 1931, a member of the committee responsible, the Very Revd. A. S. Duncan-Jones, Dean of Chichester, called a meeting of interested clergy in the diocese at which he deplored the fact that although the theologians had completed their task, nothing practical had so far come out of it. To me, Sussex-born but well aware of the limited horizons of many who live in this otherwise delightful county, such a state of affairs was not altogether surprising.

About this time I had been appointed churchwarden in the parish of Moulsecoomb on the outskirts of Brighton, and was also leader of the Youth Fellowship. Its vicar, the Revd. Bransby A. H. Jones, possessed a positive genius for 'making old things new', and for 'getting across' to English, Dutch, German and Swiss-speaking people. He seized on what the Dean had said and in 1938 took a party to Amsterdam. A Dutch party of Old Catholics returned in 1939, led by a young Pastoor, Peter Jans, later to become Bishop of Deventer. Meanwhile we made plans to take a group to Switzerland that summer. Then the war came, and all such activities had to be put aside. 'It looks bad for England!', the returning Dutch group solemnly remarked. Communication between us ended during the following year.

After six years of war, correspondence revealed that our Dutch friends were all very much alive. In Switzerland, my letters got through a strict censorship and in a short time the business of exchange trips was resumed, despite difficulties of finance and transport. The Dutch authorities at first lacked foreign exchange, so we raised funds through a local newspaper appeal and lent the first post-war party the rest which we subsequently recovered in Holland. The party for Switzerland in 1947 also had currency problems, and an early application had to be made for a group allocation, part of which had to be taken in 'travel vouchers' – available for travel, or in restaurants and cafés, but not in shops. However, sympathetic shopkeepers knew how to handle this situation. We also had visa

---

* Jack Witten died suddenly on 20 February 1982.

complications and trouble with a station bus in Paris, as well as difficulties at the passport-control; but we arrived in Basle to find the parish hall decorated with Union Jacks and Swiss cantonal flags. A pro-British speech was made by a large, emotional Swiss lady, and after singing 'God save the King' together, we tucked into our first continental breakfast of unlimited rolls, Swiss cheese and coffee. Contact was soon made with the national youth leaders in Switzerland, as well as with Pfr. Max Williman, a senior Old Catholic priest in Zurich, Pfr. Urs Küry of Olten who later succeeded his father as bishop, and Pfr. Lothar Affolter, parish priest of Solothurn a lovely town near the Jura mountains.

Contacts in both Holland and Switzerland have grown steadily since those early days. Youth exchanges continued every year until the early 1970s. They later included German Old Catholics, while our parties also went to Germany and Austria. Almost by accident we had embarked on something of great value in the relations between ourselves and the Old Catholic Churches. The Old Catholics clearly wanted to know more about us, and the appalling ignorance concerning them in England was obvious. The great work of J. M. Neale in the nineteenth century was largely unknown, and C. B. Moss had only just written his excellent book *The Old Catholic Movement*. Activities had to spread beyond the limits of a single Sussex parish and its progressive vicar. It was just then that I met the Revd. J. B. Dakin of the St. Willibrord Society committee, and its General Secretary, the Revd. John Burley. As a result, I was asked in 1950 to be the first-ever Youth Secretary, an office which I held for fourteen years. Having shortly before been appointed headmaster of a Brighton church school, I welcomed this opportunity to develop in my spare time a deeper side to our collaboration with 'co-religionists' across the Channel.

Church teaching was most necessary amongst young people and fundamental to our relations with the Old Catholic Churches. It was decided to hold an International Youth Conference in Brighton parish church and memorial hall in 1951. Sixty-seven Anglicans and forty Old Catholics attended, and some who may be called 'elder statesmen' supported the venture with their presence. These included Lord Luke, Lady Saltoun and the Bishop of Lewes, Geoffrey Warde. The Bishop of Chichester, Dr. George Bell, though prevented from attending, sent good wishes. The programme was intensive and broadly set the pattern for future conferences. Topics considered were 'The Churches in the Communist Countries' (Canon H. M. Waddams), 'The Churches in Western Europe' (Canon N. J. Cockburn, of the British and Foreign Bible Society), and 'Catholic Christians in the World of Today' (the Revd. Chad Varah, later director of 'the Samaritans'). There was an International Evening and a day excursion to Canterbury. The Bishop of Lewes celebrated the Eucharist each morning. The final session entitled 'What next?' was in the Youth Secretary's hands, and it was suggested that future conferences should be held every three years in the participating countries in turn. Anglicans would, in future, be regarded as part of the Old Catholic 'Liga'.

The Austrians at Brighton, under the leadership of Elfriede Kühnle (later Kreuzeder), were anxious to have the next conference in Vienna. However, this needed very careful consideration in view of the fact that Austria generally, and Vienna in particular, was still under four-power Allied control. My wife and I made a hair-raising journey there in 1953, but Vienna intrigued us and we resolved to bring an Anglican party there *after* the next conference which was to be held, after all, in the mountains at Saalbach. Fifty-seven young Anglicans came to this Youth Conference, which was also representative of all the countries in the Old Catholic Union of Utrecht. Some of the proceedings were broadcast on the Austrian radio and the Allied Forces' network. Subjects discussed at Saalbach concerned 'Christianity and Family Life' (Dr. Ernst Kreuzeder), 'Work' (the Revd. Chad Varah) and 'Politics' (Pfr. M. Williman). Daily Eucharists were arranged by each country in turn. Many participants commented on the warm understanding among members of this conference.

The three-year interval between the Brighton and the Saalbach conferences had proved satisfactory, and this, together with the daily Eucharist, became the agreed policy as regards the future. For some time too, we maintained an international news-sheet entitled *Internews*. The Society was greatly indebted at that period to the initiative and many new ideas which came from Elfriede Kühnle.

The next Youth Conference was held in 1957 at Woudschoten in Holland, near Utrecht. With the experience gained from its predecessors, it was splendidly organized, and the number of applicants overwhelming. Of the two hundred who assembled at Woudschoten, one hundred and seventeen were Anglicans. There was a programme-brochure in three languages, and the proceedings were recorded on tape. Messages were read from the Archbishop of Canterbury and the Bishop of Chichester. Speakers included the veteran Dr. C. B. Moss and the Revd. Chad Varah. Also in the party was the Revd. John Satterthwaite who had recently been appointed Secretary of the Church of England Council on Foreign Relations. Subjects of deeper concern in regard to our church life together were tackled at this conference, namely 'The value and significance of Catholicism today' (Dr. C. B. Moss and Professor P. J. Maan) and 'Youth obligations and opportunities in the life of the Church' (the Revd. Chad Varah and Pastoor A. J. Glazemaker). The Abbé Bekkens also spoke on the Old Catholic Mission in Paris. The daily celebration as the pattern of Eucharistic worship together culminated in a final Eucharist in St. Gertrude's Cathedral, Utrecht. Recordings made were broadcast on the Dutch world radio service. As one of the three surviving members of the Bonn Conference, Dr. Moss was admitted to membership of the Old Catholic Students' Union, 'Batavia', in Holland – a very rare and special honour for a foreigner.

Plans for the 1960 Youth Conference to be held in Switzerland were slow in getting off the ground. Solothurn would have been the ideal centre, but the conference eventually found a home in an army training barracks for officers at Bretaye, situated in the mountains high above Villars. We found out later that many of the Swiss youngsters did not even know it was taking place! Only one German arrived. The Anglican numbered forty-six, the Dutch had a fair-sized group, and half-a-dozen came from Austria. Pfr. Gottfried Konrad made himself responsible for all the organization, and the cooking was in the hands of two men from his parish. Despite setbacks, we covered a lot of ground at the Bretaye conference, as the list of subjects discussed shows: 'As sheep among wolves' (Pfr. Fluckiger from Solothurn), 'What does the World expect of the Churches?' (the Revd. M. Halliwell), 'Destruction of Religion' (the Revd. Dewi Morgan) and 'Foreign Mission' (Pastoor Teun Horstmann).

After the near disaster of Bretaye it was a bold move to decide to have the next conference in Germany in 1963. After much correspondence with the authorities concerned (Professor Küppers at the seminary in Bonn, and Pfr. Pursch), and with considerable help from Pfr. Sigisbert Kraft of Karlsruhe, it was agreed to hold the conference in the Burg Stahleck, a restored medieval castle high above the Rhine at Bacharach, now used as a youth hostel. The

English group numbered sixty but there were seventy Old Catholics. The German group was large through the efforts of Pfr. Kraft and Professor Küppers, and there was a sizeable number from Holland and a few from Austria and Switzerland. Speakers included the Revd. Michael Bruce a prominent member of the Church Assembly, and Brother Williams, SSF, the theme of the conference being 'Ye shall be my witnesses'. Professor Küppers' opening address was outstanding. In a messege sent to the conference Archbishop Ramsey spoke of the need to see more clearly that God was calling the members to promote the unity of the Church in holiness, in truth and in love. In the dark one evening, a service of dedication with intercessions for world peace was held in a ruined chapel. Bishop Demmel was the celebrant at the final Eucharist.

After Bacharach it seemed to me that the time had come for a change as regards Youth leadership in the Society. We had had a considerable number of exchange trips involving some two thousand young people, had held a conference in each country in turn, and had made a vast number of friends, clerical and lay. The Revd. John Burley wished to resign as General Secretary because of the work involved in a large parish to which he had recently moved. Pressure was being put on me to take his place but a compromise was reached. John Burley would continue to look after clerical affairs, while I undertook a new post as Lay Secretary and became an assessor on the Foreign Relations Old Catholic committee. Ann Clayton took over as Youth Secretary until she married and moved to Cologne some years later.

'The Church looks forward' was the title of the first of the second round of conferences, held in 1966, appropriately enough, in Christ Church College of Education, Canterbury. There was a brochure with a conference 'Who's Who', listing twenty prominent church leaders who had key parts to play. Julia Butterworth, now deaconess at Canterbury Cathedral, was official interpreter. Themes covered were 'The Church's Worship' (the Rt. Revd. John Hughes, Bishop of Croydon), 'Church and Family Life' (Pfr. S. Kraft), 'Church and Mission' (Pastoor F. Smit) and 'Unity of the Church' (Canon H. M. Waddams). The International Evening was one of the best ever, enlivened by Sigisbert Kraft impersonating the fifth Beatle, complete with guitar and outrageous hair-style![12] Only fifty Anglicans were present at this conference as compared with ninety Old Catholics. Despite wide advertisement, and after allowing for Old Catholic euphoria where Canterbury was concerned, there was a very real impression that youth work in Anglican parishes was falling apart, although the quality of those who did attend was of the best.

One more conference was held: this time at St. Pölten in Austria in August 1969. It became increasingly obvious during the preparations that either the so-called 'generation gap', or the arrival of the permissive society and the inward-looking attitude of so many parishes were combining to work against what had hitherto been done with some success. The theme of the 1969 conference was 'Old Church in a New Age', the Revd. John Bowker and his wife being the Anglican speakers. Despite extensive advertisement once again, only thirty Anglicans came to what proved to be the last Youth Conference of the series which had started eighteen years before. To be fair, St. Pölten was a considerable journey; nor were the Old Catholics so fortunate on this occasion. There was, as always, a good Dutch contingent, and there were small groups from Austria and Germany; but no Swiss appeared, nor did their speaker when he learnt of the situation!

Let nobody doubt however, that this activity on behalf of the youth has done much towards reviving the Society of St. Willibrord, as well as forwarding the objects of the Bonn Agreement. The jubilee in 1981 revealed that there is something of a youth revival in Holland, and also in Switzerland and Germany, with a desire to pick up the threads again. Nevertheless, the discovery made at St. Pölten that youngsters now preferred to be housed together at some conference centre or similar building rather than in separate families, suggests that future conferences may have to take on a new look.

One of the jobs of the Lay Secretary was to set up sixteen area representatives in England, and also secretaries for Scotland, Wales and Ireland. We were greatly helped by members of former youth parties who have kept in touch with those interested in the Society in their areas, distributing news-letters, holding occasional meetings and reporting on changes of addresses. There are also representatives in Australia, South Africa, the USA and Canada.

My wife and I formed the habit of a continental tour each August, which included visits to many Old Catholic centres. From 1964 onwards we took our car, and have covered over 35,000 miles in this way.[13] All this happy journeying has contributed to the building up of Anglican-Old Catholic relations. Mrs. Nancy Stamp, our excellent members' treasurer, began her duties in 1966. The International

Ecumenical Fellowship was founded in 1967, and one of those who helped to bring it into being, the Revd. Michael Bruce, was a member of the SSW and worked constantly for Christian unity until his untimely death in the following year. We moved to Haywards Heath in 1955 when I was appointed to the headship of St. Wilfrid's Church of England school, remaining in that post until retirement in 1969, bringing, as I hoped, a good many years ahead to pursue other interests, not least within the Society of St. Willibrord.

Until their duties made it impossible, successive Bishops of Fulham (later with Gibraltar) served as chairman of the Society's Executive committee. Canon Frederick Hood, chancellor of St. Paul's Cathedral, took over this function in the 1960s, and he was succeeded by Prebendary Henry Cooper, rector of Bloomsbury and a prominent member of the Church Assembly.

I was able to attend the Old Catholic Congress at Bonn in September 1970, in association with the centenary of the Union of Utrecht and the work of Ignaz Döllinger, whose name is perpetuated in the Studentheim in the Baumschulallee, also in Bonn. The Congress revealed a lively state of affairs in the Old Catholic Churches. There were some seven hundred delegates, including over sixty priests and twelve bishops. About twenty countries were represented. Some of the young people present were making a protest of conscience at world affairs; but they had not opted out of spiritual life or participation in the worship of their churches. The Congress ended with an inspiring Eucharist, concelebrated by all the bishops and priests present, and under blazing television lights. In contrast at this time, the Anglican branch of the Society was going through a somewhat traumatic re-appraisal of its place in a rapidly changing scene. Many clergy seemed unable to cope with the so-called 'new morality', or the use of 'industrial muscle' for purely secular interests. Church youth service, as one knew it up to the 1950s and 1960s, simply disappeared, although everyone applauded when youngsters took part in non-ecclesiastical activities on behalf of charitable causes – even during the hours of public worship on Sundays!

Happily, a new look Annual General Meeting in 1972 brought fresh life to the Society. It was agreed to hold a festival on the Saturday nearest to St. Willibrord's day (7 November) at the church of St. Andrew-by-the-Wardrobe in the City of London, by invitation of its rector, the Revd. F. P. Coleman, a senior member of the committee. The Bishop of Haarlem (Mgr. G. A. van Kleef), an old friend, celebrated the Dutch liturgy. About forty-five members attended, and later heard Bishop van Kleef speak on ecumenical affairs. The festival has been held every year since then and has brought distinguished overseas guests to various London churches. Attendance has grown slowly but steadily.

The normal work of the SSW continued until 1974, when Canon John Burley announced that he would be retiring in the following year. At the same time, the Society's finances were suffering – partly owing to inflation, though there was also a feeling in some areas that it had perhaps outlived its usefulness. Matters were discussed with the continental section, especially with Peggy van Vliet, a redoubtable worker on the Society's behalf, and with the Bishop of Haarlem. It was unanimously agreed that the Society had much to do in the future: an opinion reinforced by Bishop John Satterthwaite, who preached a challenging sermon at the 1975 festival. The Executive Committee allowed me to form a 'working party' to investigate the situation and to make new plans for the future. The impetus created by this pooling of ideas is still with us. There was a thorough discussion, wide-ranging plans were made, and some new officers and committee members were enlisted. Canon Burley retired at the autumn festival in 1975 and was succeeded by the Revd. Michael Woodgate, vicar of St. Peter's Streatham, and a former member of the youth parties of the late 1950s. The Revd. C. J. Klyberg took over as editor of the News-letter, which was given a new format and an extended coverage of news. The Society had full support from Canon Michael Moore, Bishop Satterthwaite's successor as Secretary of the Council on Foreign Relations. A new chapter had opened.

In 1975 news suddenly came that the Society was to receive a sizeable legacy from the estate of the late Miss Helen Loddiges. This transformed its financial situation almost at a stroke. For the first time it was able to give a reception to the members of the Anglican-Old Catholic Theological Conference which, in 1976, was held at the Bishop's Palace, Chichester. Distinguished visiting speakers could now be invited to the annual festival, and there was a further enlargement of the News-letter. On the appointment of Fr. Klyberg as Dean of Lusaka, the Revd. Phillip Swingler took over its editorship at short notice. Ill health regrettably prevented him from continuing, but waiting in the wings, as it were, was the Revd. Alan Cole, recently returned to England from Australia. As chaplain to Ardingly

College he was near at hand and the Society's debt to him is immeasurable. Already he was minutes' secretary to the committee, and he later 'masterminded' the production of this Jubilee book, working closely with the editor and publisher. Fr. Cole became Anglican chaplain in Bonn and Cologne at the beginning of 1982, but is continuing as editor of the News-letter from a position well situated for gathering news from the continent.

Sadly, in 1977, Prebendary Henry Cooper, who had been an inspiring chairman of the Executive Committee, retired. Bishop John Satterthwaite, as the Society's chairman, then invited me to take over from him. I felt that this was a post for someone in the higher ranks of the clergy; but my objections were overcome when the bishop reminded me of my long associations with the SSW, and of my extensive knowledge of Old Catholic affairs. The task of leading the committee in an expanding situation is an enjoyable one. From time to time Old Catholic visitors are welcomed at the Executive Committee: among them, Mrs. Peggy van Vliet, General Secretary of the Old Catholic section of the Society, and Mr. Laurence Orzell of the Polish National Catholic Church of America and a contributor to this volume.

Prebendary Cooper and Canon Burley were honoured with Life Membership in 1978 as well as the Revd. Bransby A. H. Jones for his pioneering work in the early days of youth exchange visits. In May of that year the Old Catholic Congress was held at Noordwyherhout in Holland. There was a much stronger Anglican respresentation consisting of the Bishop of Chichester (representing the Archbishop of Canterbury), Bishop John Satterthwaite, the Bishop of Kentucky and a number of clergy and members of the religious orders. Regrettably, only two lay members were free to attend. A large number of Old Catholic young people took part. In contrast, there seems to be an increasing lack of interest in these activities on the part of Anglican youngsters. When one sees their deep involvement in other concerns, one feels very troubled that the churches in this country do not do better in an ever-growing pagan/humanist society.

Dr. Andreas Rinkel, former Archbishop of Utrecht, died at the age of ninety on 26 March 1979, and Professor Johannes Zeimet of Karlsruhe a few weeks later. They were great and much loved leaders in the Old Catholic Churches of the Netherlands and Germany. The summer of that year was specially memorable for the large number of Old Catholics who descended on English shores, including two groups of Austrians led respectively by Bishop Hummel and Dr. Elfriede Kreuzeder. A youth group from Wiesbaden visited York and later came on to Haywards Heath in Sussex. The enthronement of Robert Runcie as Archbishop of Canterbury on 25 March 1980 was a very uplifting occasion, and the Society of St. Willibrord scored high praise for the support it gave in arranging hospitality for the Old Catholic representatives who attended. These were Archbishop Kok of Utrecht, Bishop Brinkues from Germany, Bishop Hummel from Austria, Prime Bishop Thaddeus Majewksi of the National Catholic Church of Poland, with his chaplain Fr. Edward Balakier, and Mrs. Peggy van Vliet from Holland.

The jubilee of the Bonn Agreement took place in 1981, and already, ahead of the official celebrations in July, the Old Catholic Churches were showing a lively interest. In Switzerland there was a highly imaginative and well-supported event, which began with a Eucharist for Anglicans and Old Catholics in Lausanne, followed by an excursion by boat on the Lake of Geneva with lunch on board, and then Evensong in St. John's Territet. On the return journey there was music and singing, and official messages of greeting were read, including one from the Society. Over two hundred people shared in this. In Germany too, the Old Catholics had already celebrated the jubilee on 3 May when one of the Society's members, the Revd. J. M. Brotherton rural dean of Oxford, visiting Bonn was invited to concelebrate the Eucharist with Bishop Brinkhues, Pfr. Pursch the parish priest, and others. This event was well publicised in the local press for the cause of intercommunion.

In England the Society of St. Willibrord had special responsibilities for seeing that the jubilee was well observed. It was agreed to have a festival Eucharist in Westminster Abbey concelebrated by the Archbishops of Canterbury and Utrecht on Thursday 2 July, the exact anniversary date of the Agreement, followed by a lecture given in Church House by the Bishop of Chichester and a buffet lunch. At Utrecht a final celebration was held on 7 November, St. Willibrord's day with the same concelebrants. Both occasions drew large numbers of supporters. Through the excellent publicity arrangements, particularly on the part of Mr. John Miles of the Church Information Office, the attendance at Westminster Abbey exceeded all expectations – though the indifference shown by the national press and media, with the exception of *The Times* and local radio in the London area, cannot be allowed to pass without comment. All this,

1. St. Gertrude's Cathedral, Utrecht

2. Cardinal Alfrink and Archbishop Rinkel, 7 November 1966

3. The Consecration of Bishop Glazemaker, 1979

4. Archbishop Kok and Archbishop Runcie, 2 July 1981

and much more, is recorded in the minutes of the Executive Committee and our News-letter. What a contrast it makes to the narrow confines of earlier times!

I am confident that in the Society of St. Willibrord we are now keeping faith with the Dean of Chichester of fifty years ago in getting on with the practical aspects of the Bonn Agreement. We are well supported at Lambeth and by Bishop John Satterthwaite; our News-letter is praised far and wide; the Society is growing, and the Executive Committee is bringing together those who have special gifts to offer.

Finally, tribute must be paid to all those who, through many contacts during the past thirty-five years since the publication of *The Old Catholic Movement* by Dr. Moss, have worked to promote the activities of the Society in this country and overseas.

NOTES

1. Gordon Huelin, *St. Willibrord and his Society*, p. 51.
2. ibid., p. 55.
3. A full account of this strange figure can be found in C. B. Moss, *The Old Catholic Movement*, pp. 298–304.
4. Gordon Huelin, op. cit., p. 55.
5. ibid., p. 57.
6. In what follows, use has been made on the Minutes of the Society of St. Willibrord.
7. An account of these meetings, together with the important resolution (35) of the Lambeth Conference requesting the appointment of a Commission can be found in C. B . Moss, op. cit., Ch. 28.
8. For the agreed terms of Intercommunion, see Appendix I.
9. J. G. Lockhart, *Cosmo Gordon Lang*, p. 365: 'through the participation of Old Catholic Bishops in Anglican Consecrations . . . the ministerial succession of the Episcopate of the Old Catholics began to be merged with that of the Church of England'.
10. Gordon Huelin, op. cit., p. 68.
11. ibid., pp. 73–4.
12. The four Beatles were a celebrated English 'pop' group, much in the news at that time.
13. John Burley referred to us as 'ambassadors at large for the Society, free from departmental duties'!

6

The Old Catholic Liturgies

Petrus Maan

The history of the Old Catholic liturgies is a thrilling one, for in its liturgy one hears the heart-beat of the Church.

It is important to remember that the Dutch Old Catholics did not call themselves 'Old Catholic' until the end of the nineteenth century. Before that time they preferred the name 'Roman Catholic, adhering to the ancient episcopal clergy' (Rooms-Katholieken van de Oud-Bisschoppelijke Clerezie). In accordance with this title, they kept strictly to Roman Catholic rites, though, of course, they had their own characteristics. For example, they laid much stress on Bible reading and published their own translation of the Holy Scriptures. But in their worship in church they followed the Roman Missal of the council of Trent, and forgot that there had ever been a Utrecht Missal. They translated the Roman Missal into Dutch, and published a book in seven parts with all the lessons and gospels, plus notes upon each reading. No wonder that every member of the Church of Utrecht needed his or her own place in the church, where all this library of books would be kept for use on the appropriate Sunday! Another characteristic of the Church of Utrecht in the seventeenth century was that the whole liturgy, including the entire Prayer of Consecration, was said loudly and distinctly by the priest. Another, that in administering Baptism and other sacraments, the Dutch language was used. On Sunday afternoons, Vespers was sung in Latin. The calendar of the saints was taken from the Roman Missal. The only difference was that the festival of St. Boniface was celebrated on 5 July because the original day (5 June) coincided with the octave of Corpus Christi. The breviary used was the Paris Breviary, with an appendix for the Dutch province.

We leave the Dutch Church for the moment, and turn to the Old Catholic movement in Germany in the seventies of the nineteenth century. As parishes came into existence here, more or less unwillingly, the question of liturgy naturally arose. It was a difficult problem to solve, because many people who were anti-Roman did not as yet realize what it would mean to be an Old Catholic. There were turbulent discussions on the use of liturgical vestments, on the use of plainsong, on the use of Latin in public worship, and so on. Fortunately the leading figures of the movement showed great prudence, and found the right way through the maze. They knew the real grievances of the people, who objected to private masses where no faithful were present, and to masses for which fees were paid. They protested against services which they could not understand, and against fasting regulations which had lost their meaning.

In 1875 the second German Synod published a Ritual, edited by Professor Reusch, with the administration of the sacraments in the German language. In 1877 the fourth Synod decreed that Parish Communion every Sunday should be the rule; that private masses should be abolished, and the faithful should always be represented at the Eucharist; that a requiem should be celebrated only once, and commemoration services should be held only when family or friends of the deceased were present, and that every celebration of the Eucharist should be a sign of the community: priest and people belong together. From 1880 the German language was permitted for some parts of the Eucharist.

In the same year there was an important development in the Christ Catholic Church of Switzerland. The Church published an Order for the Eucharist of which Bishop Eduard Herzog was the compiler. It was a tremendous event in that it was not a translation of the Roman Missal, but an independent creation. Bishop Herzog was originally a New Testament scholar with a great sense of what catholicity means and with a strong pastoral insight. Anglicans looking back upon the work of Cranmer may wish to differ, but Bishop Herzog's *Book of Prayer* has been called 'the most beautiful present ever given by a bishop to his church'. The Eucharist is based upon the Roman Missal, with a clearly drawn distinction between the Service of the Word and the Celebration of the Holy Supper. In the latter part there is a new influence of Biblical insights, especially from the Gospel according to St. John and the Epistle to the Hebrews. The influence of the ancient eastern liturgies is also seen, in that Bishop Herzog introduced the epiclesis into his rite. This prayer to the Holy Spirit is a feature of Eastern liturgies, but up to this time had been found in the West only in the English rite of 1549 and the Scottish Episcopal rite of 1637. It was also in the English Non-jurors' rite, but this had no official standing. Herzog placed his epiclesis before the words of Institution. The fact that Bishop Herzog introduced the epiclesis into his order of the Eucharist had a great impact on Old Catholic worship and theology.

Bishop Herzog had the co-operation of Professor A. Thürlings, who was a specialist in liturgics and hymnology, and thus it was possible for the Prayer and Hymn Books to be published together. As well as the epiclesis, there was another innovation in the Herzog Prayer Book, in that it gave the people the opportunity to sing the psalms in German and in plainsong. The production of this Prayer Book was indeed a major event in the history of the Christ Catholic Church of Switzerland, and set a course for the other Old Catholic Churches to follow.

To return to Germany again, the authorities there invited Professor Thürlings to take charge of the publication of the German Order for the Eucharist. It came out in 1885, accompanied by a book of more than two hundred hymns. The liturgy follows the Roman Missal more closely than the Swiss Eucharist does, and is distinguished by the beauty of the German. Following where Bishop Herzog had led, Dr. Thürlings inserted the epiclesis before the words of Institution.

The Old Catholic Church in Austria in her liturgy followed the lead of the German Church.

The Church of Utrecht was rather startled by the suddenness with which these developments in worship took place in the churches of Switzerland, Germany and Austria. It is understandable that in the Netherlands too there grew an ever-stronger desire for a vernacular liturgy. On the other hand, the bishops were reluctant to accept one because they did not want to emphasize their differences with the Papal Roman Catholics. So it came about that only in the twentieth century was the great decision taken: first there appeared a translation of Vespers with psalms, hymns and prayers for all Sundays and festival days throughout the year. The psalms were to be sung in plainsong. There were also forms for a service of sacramental benediction, for New Year's Day, and for special services during Lent.

In 1911 the Dutch translation of the Mass was finally ready. There were only minor changes from the text of the Roman Missal. For example, there was no mention of the Pope in the intercessions, and the catalogue of saints appears according to the Roman rite. For each

Sunday and festival there was an introit sung at the beginning of the service according to Dutch custom. There were no graduals, offertoriums, or communion texts, but there are sequences after the Epistle on Easter Day, Pentecost, Corpus Christi, and in the Requiem. There are twenty-two Prefaces – many more than in the Roman Missal. This 'Misboek' had a good reception by the faithful, and was soon accompanied by books for the hymns and plainchant parts of the liturgy.

After World War II there was a strong movement for the reform of the liturgy. Renewed ecumenical contacts (in particular, Anglican, Eastern Orthodox, Taizé) made it imperative to raise questions about it. At every conference of Old Catholic theologians there were papers on this subject. These discussed the idea of sacrifice, the atonement, representation, participation, the real presence, priesthood, and so on. There was even a plan considered for a common order of the Eucharist to be used by all Old Catholic Churches, but this ideal has never been attained. One may ask if the principle of the independence of national churches as held by Anglicans and Old Catholics should also apply to the liturgy. Apparently the churches of the Anglican Communion have decided it should, and by default the Old Catholics have done the same.

The Reverend Kurt Pursch of the Old Catholic Seminary in Bonn published a new missal that kept close to Thürlings', but paid special attention to the text and music of introit, gradual, offertory and communion texts.

Ten years later a totally new order of the Eucharist was authorized. It lays emphasis on intercessory prayer, an Anglican influence. In the Eucharistic rite itself it shows the influence of the liturgy of Hippolytus in stressing salvation history. The epiclesis is introduced for the first time in the Netherlands, but in contrast with the usage in Germany and Switzerland it appears after the words of Institution. This liturgy was very well designed, and has had a good reception by both old and young among the faithful. At the same time a revision of the old text of the Roman Missal was published in a new translation and without secondary additions. Here are the Eucharistic Prayer and Canon from the new or 'Second Order of the Mass according to the use of the Old Catholic Church in the Netherlands':

EUCHARISTIC PRAYER

The congregation stand.
The Lord be with you.
And with thy spirit.
Lift up your hearts.
We lift them up unto the Lord.
Let us give thanks unto the Lord our God.
It is meet and right so to do.

With our whole heart do we give thanks continually,
Lord, holy Father, almighty, everlasting God,
who art worthy to receive honour and power.

For heaven and earth and all that is,
the visible and the invisible,
thou hast created through thy Word.

As the crown of thy creation
thou didst make man in thine own image,
and hast given him to share wondrously
in thy greatness.

We thank thee that thy merciful kindness is over us
by day and by night,
and that thou wilt be with us in all our ways.

Blessed art thou for all
that thou in thy great mercy hast done for us.
Thy mercy endures from generation to generation.

In our forefather Abraham thou hast given us
the promise of thy salvation,
and upon Israel thy servant thou hadst mercy.

By thy prophets thou hast spoken to us.
Thou hast visited thy people
and declared their redemption.

And in fulfilment of thy promises
thou didst send unto us thy beloved Son,
Jesus Christ, our Redeemer and Saviour.

Through him we glorify and praise thee
with all the heavenly hosts,
and with all thy chosen, who stand around thy throne
confessing in deep reverence:

Holy, holy, holy, Lord God of hosts,
Heaven and earth are full of thy glory.
Hosanna in the highest.
Blessed ✠ is he that cometh in the Name of the Lord.
Hosanna in the highest.

THE CANON

The congregation kneel and the priest says:

Blessed art thou, Lord of all majesty
and King of eternal glory,
through Jesus Christ, thine only begotten Son.

In him thy Word was made flesh
and the fullness of thy grace shone forth splendidly.
In all things he fulfilled thy will
and glorified thy Name.

He proclaimed thy kingdom to us
and broke for us the power of darkness.

Our guilt he took upon himself,
he reconciled us to thee
and unlocked the new paradise for us.

As the way, the truth and the life
has he revealed us thy love.
And therein was he obedient to thee
unto the end,
even unto the Cross,
that he might destroy death by his death
and by his rising restore our life.

On the night in which of his own free will
he gave himself up,
he took the bread in his hands
and with his eyes lifted up to thee his heavenly Father
he gave thanks, blessed it,
broke it
and gave it to his disciples, saying:
Take, eat; this is my body,
which is given for you ✠.

Likewise after supper he took the cup;
gave thanks to thee, blessed it
and gave it to his disciples, saying:

Drink ye all of this;
This is my blood of the new covenant,
which is shed for you and for many
for the remission of sins ✠.
As oft as ye do this,
Ye shall do it in remembrance of me.
Therefore, O Lord, remembering his saving passion,
his glorious resurrection
and his exaltation to thy right hand,

and looking for his coming in the fullness of majesty,
we here set forth this sign of our faith in him,
who offered the perfect sacrifice to thee
and gained an eternal salvation for us.
Send then, we pray thee, thy Holy Spirit,
the giver of all life and sanctification,
upon us and upon these thy gifts:
bread and wine of eternal life.
And take them from our hands
as a sacrifice acceptable to thee,
by which we offer ourselves to thee,
so that the bread which we break
is a sharing of the body of thy Son
and the cup which we bless
is a sharing of the blood of thy Son.
Grant that all who partake of thy heavenly altar,
may evermore remain united with thee,
together with all thy saints and chosen ones,
with thy blessed and glorious handmaiden
Mary, the mother of our Lord,
(with St. ......, whose memory we keep today)
with thy prophets and apostles,
with thy martyrs and confessors
and with all, who in thy kingdom
stand around thy throne in praise and prayer.

*If the memorials following for the departed and for
the living have taken place at the Intercession, they
may be omitted here.*

(Grant, Lord, also a share in the glory
to the departed, whom each of us wishes
to remember before thee . . .
Deal with them and all men according
to thy merciful kindness
and let perpetual light shine upon them.
Remember also thy servants on earth
for whom we invoke thy mercy . . .)

Bless thy Church throughout the world
and grant it unity and peace.
Renew the earth according to thy promise,
remember all peoples
and grant that all men
may give thee thanks and worship
and laud thy holy name.

Through thy beloved Son, our Lord, Jesus Christ
with whom and in whom, almighty Father,
in the unity of the Holy Spirit,
all honour and majesty, power and glory be unto thee,
now and throughout all ages, world without end.
Amen.[1]

The Synod of the Christ Catholic Church in Switzerland decided in 1957 to prepare a new edition of their Prayer Book. Professor A. E. Ruthy of Berne University led this enterprise. With his assistants he collected much material and in 1978 the new order for the celebration of the Eucharist appeared, along with a revised hymn book. In the former, four parts of the eucharistic meal are emphasized: the Word, the Meal, the Thanksgiving, and Mission. In Switzerland the Prayer Book has to be provided in both French and German.

The use of Polish in the liturgy of the PNCC developed gradually, owing partly to the lack of translations in the vernacular. Bishop Hodur tried to have these produced by several scholarly clergy, but reserved to himself the right of deciding the final form. He himself used manuscript books for many years in his Scranton congregation. Some of these were known as 'Bishop Hodur's paraphrases'. In most cases they were fairly close translations of the Tridentine Roman rite, with slight omissions such as the prayers for the Pope. In the course of time it became possible to obtain printed books for the congregations. In March 1973 there appeared the PNCC revised order which has become the official liturgy throughout the church. It is called in English *The Holy Sacrifice of the Mass and Distribution of Holy Communion*, and is largely the work of Bishop Zielinski, Prime Bishop Emeritus. It is basically a conservative revision of the Roman Mass of 1570, with the Asperges before the High Mass, and an opening penitential rite similar to that of the reformed Roman liturgy, but with a longer confession of sin. The traditional Canon, or that of Bishop Hodur, may be used, and Bishop Zielinski has recently gone so far as to suggest still another option – the Canon of Hippolytus. As well as stressing the fact that the offering of the Eucharist should not be separated from the reception of the Gifts, thus advocating frequent communion, the observance of the pre-communion fast is suggested, at least for two hours before reception, if not from the previous midnight. The term 'transubstantiation' is not used, but the Real Presence 'under the species of bread and wine' is taught very clearly, and the Eucharist is considered 'a true sac-rifice'. The Holy Communion is administered in one of three ways: under the species of bread alone; under both species individually; and by intinction. The last of these seems to be the most common custom. At the end of the Eucharist, the 'Last Gospel' may still be used, and the old Roman after-Mass devotions, if the people express a desire for them.

Extra-liturgical devotion, such as the Benediction of the Blessed Sacrament, is common. This often takes place on Sunday after High Mass. A modified form of Vespers with Benediction is found in some congregations. Some congregations use Bishop Hodur's adaptation of Tenebrae during Holy Week. Polish Catholics are very fond of litanies, and those of the Blessed Virgin Mary are used in May and October, and of the Sacred Heart in June. These texts have changed very little from those of Polish Roman Catholic usage of years gone by. There is one more popular Passiontide devotion to be mentioned, known as 'Bitter Lamentations', consisting of prayer, recollections, penitential hymns and responses. It is of Jesuit origin, as are the litanies mentioned above. The devotion of the PNCC is greatly influenced by Jesuit developments, in contrast to the devotion of the Church of Utrecht, which has no room for Jesuit influence anywhere.

Again it will be seen how much more conservative the PNCC is in its devotion than are European Old Catholics when one looks at the dedication of their churches. Among the PNCC these are often dedicated to the Sacred Heart of Jesus, the Holy Mother of the Rosary, and there is even one to the Immaculate Conception. Counter-Reformation piety holds a much stronger sway over the members of the PNCC than over the Old Catholics of Europe.

As far back as 1931 Bishop Hodur advocated celebration of the Eucharist facing the people, and most of the churches which have high altars against the east wall also have one free-standing altar at which the celebrant may do as Bishop Hodur suggested. However, in some other respects the PNCC buildings are pre-Vatican II, with holy water stoup and confessional boxes, while the vestments used are the fiddle-back style, and albs and cottas are well decorated with lace. On the other hand English is used in the liturgy, and the Polish patriotic commemorations have been reduced in number and im-portance. Names without special Christian significance have been removed from the calendar. In common with the other Old Catholic Churches and the Eastern Orthodox Churches, the *Filioque* clause is omitted from the Nicene Creed. Liturgically, the Polish Catholic Church follows a similar pattern to that of the PNCC.

There is no new information to hand on the liturgies of the Austrian, Czechoslovak and Yugoslav Churches.

On the international level, the Bishops' Conference has asked for a new order for ordination. This means an expedition into totally new fields of study in ministry, priesthood and episcopacy. It may be said that the work of liturgical study and revision will never end.

NOTE

1. *Eucharistic Worship – Old Catholic Church of the Netherlands*, pp. 32–5.

7

Old Catholic Spirituality

JAN VISSER

It is difficult to write or speak about Old Catholic spirituality. The reason for this is that 'Old Catholic spirituality' suggests a specific species of the spiritual life which can be described as typically 'Old Catholic'. This presupposes that all congregations which call themselves Old Catholic can be characterised by the same kind of spiritual life and life-style.

This is certainly not the case. In the various Old Catholic Churches and in the various parishes there is a different style of spiritual life. Everyone who visits Old Catholic parishes in Holland, Germany, Switzerland and Poland would be confronted by different liturgies, devotions, spiritual life-styles and mentalities. This is by no means surprising. Every Old Catholic community is rooted in its own, specific historical situation. They arose at different times. They were brought about by different issues. But there is more to it than that. It should also be said that Old Catholic ecclesiology actually legitimates these differences. To put it bluntly: Old Catholics stand for the autonomy of local churches. This means that they tolerate in the one church spread out all over the world different styles of life according to the specific situation in which the church happens to be living. This typically Old Catholic ecclesiological principle of diversity in unity leads to different styles of life, in accordance with the famous words ascribed to St. Augustine: *in necessariis unitas, in dubiis libertas, in omnibus caritas*. These words became the motto of the German Catholics who protested against the decisions of the First Vatican Council in 1870. The differences are not so wide that there are no common elements which can be discovered. On the surface it is possible to see diversity, but, at the level of spiritual inspiration, there is indeed much common ground to be found.

So it is necessary to describe first the differences between the various styles of Old Catholic spirituality which can be found in the various national churches. Secondly, it should be noted that these differences are historically rooted in specific historical circumstances. Thirdly, we need to ask: What are the common elements in Old Catholic spirituality? The first and the last parts of this description will be rather condensed. The second part will be more extensive.

Roughly speaking, the Old Catholic Churches can be divided into three categories according to the point in time at which they first arose. So one can distinguish between the Old Catholic communities which came into being before 1870 (i.e. the First Vatican Council) and those which came into being as a result of the decisions of the First Vatican Council, and also between those which came into being as a result of certain decisions which were made on the basis of papal authority.

To the first category belongs the so-called Church of Utrecht, which came into being at the beginning of the eighteenth century. The immediate cause in this particular case was the dismissal of the Dutch bishop by the authorities of the church in Rome, and the nomination of a successor without consulting the so-called Chapter of Utrecht. The background to these historical events was bound up with considerable differences of opinion on certain theological, pastoral and moral questions to which the label 'Jansenistic' is commonly applied.

To the second category belong those churches which emerged out of the protest by theologians and laymen against the decrees of the First Vatican Council. The leaders were the German Catholics. They were followed by a Swiss movement. Subsequently, they were joined by yet more movements in the Austrian Empire.

To the third category belong the Polish National churches which originated at the turn of the century. They came into being in the United States of America where Polish immigrants were forced to accept Irish bishops. They protested against decisions of the Roman Catholic Church. Inspired by a certain priest called Hodur, they formed their own ecclesial communities. Hodur carried through certain reforms in discipline, liturgy and teachings. Afterwards, they planted a similar church in their own homeland, Poland.

The spirituality of the church of Utrecht was determined by the Catholic restoration after the Reformation. Above all, the French renewal in the second part of the seventeenth century provided the sources of inspiration for many Dutch priests and laypeople.

The spiritual renewal in the Old Catholic communities in Germany, Switzerland and the Austro-Hungarian Empire was determined by the ideals of what is usually called 'Enlightenment Catholicism'. Hence its strong, classical impact. The Polish National churches are rooted in the specific Polish tradition of Catholicism. Apparently, their rejection of a centralized papal authority determines their ecclesiastical autonomy. To a great extent, they retained their typically Polish devotions, but, because they fervently wanted to retain their Polish identity as an autonomous emigrant-church, they ultimately broke with Rome. In this connection, the so-called Mariavite Church should also be mentioned. Even more than the Polish National Church, it is characterized by its typically Polish spirituality: a combination of affective love and social feeling.

Recent studies have confirmed the substantial influence of French theologians on the conflict between Rome and Utrecht at the beginning of the eighteenth century. Such influence was not just confined to matters of ecclesiastical jurisdiction. Even theological and spiritual ideals were based upon French models. Bishop van Neercassel, the Apostolic Vicar in the second half of the seventeenth century, had a great admiration for Bossuet; and he preferred priests educated by the Oratorium to those educated in other institutes. So, numerous leading figures in the Dutch Catholic Church were educated by Oratorians, many of whom were secular clergy. Not only van Neercassel was interested in this priestly movement and its distinctive spirituality. One of his predecessors, Rovenius, even cherished a plan to found such a house in the Netherlands. He corresponded about his ideas with Jansenius. But he was not only enthusiastic about the education of priests. He was also striving to provide his church (which was then living a kind of 'underground' existence amidst the political circumstances of those times) with the inspiration of a new kind of spirituality in accordance with the renewal of the Catholic Church which followed the Council of Trent. He turned for his inspiration to the first generation of the new Jesuit order: to mostly Spanish, Italian, and German writers. His second greatest source of inspiration was French: namely François de Sales. The distinguishing marks of this kind of spiritual life were the ideals of a late medieval movement which arose in the Netherlands: the so-called *devotio moderna*. It tries to foster a real spiritual life within the context of a normal social life. A step-by-step method of meditation and asceticism was also developed. The reading of the Holy Scriptures was also emphasized.

After the Reformation, Dutch Catholics no longer had an opportunity to lead a monastic life. Monasteries were forbidden. So this kind of devotion and spirituality was welcomed by priestly chapters and communities of pious women who lived a common life like the Beguines. The priests generally derived their inspiration from the French Oratory which was founded by Pierre de Bérulle. Their pastoralia were influenced by Charles Borromeo, the great Archbishop of Milan. Their devotions were, therefore, rather sober and restricted to the basic essentials of the Christian life: to the ideal of a devotional discipline in accordance with the inspiration of the bishop. What is characteristic of this kind of spirituality is this: leading a devotional life in the midst of one's social obligations, a life lived (in secrecy) in communion with the Lord accompanied by the highest personal standards. But this tendency towards individualism was balanced by ecclesiastical discipline: and above all by the attendance at Mass and Vespers. In this way, individual piety is combined with a sense of obligation to the liturgical community. This kind of spirituality which linked the first and the second halves of the seventeenth century, is typical of the prayer-book which was written by van Neercassel under the influence of certain French models. This particular prayer-book was re-edited for the last time during the closing decade of the nineteenth century; but with certain alterations.

In this book, we can find many personal exercises and prayers for individual use, together with a translation of the liturgical texts of the Eucharist and the other sacraments. Every one of the sacraments is introduced by a short catechetical instruction and an admonition to prepare oneself to receive the sacramental grace fruitfully. The importance of a right intention is also emphasized. The distinguishing marks are well known: to be pious in one's daily life; to live in accordance with one's social state as man and woman, husband and wife; as master or servant (in modesty); not to strive after profound mystical experiences which are dangerous, (a reaction against the so-called Spanish *illuminati*); the characteristic emphasis being upon an ascetic style of life. The aim is to control the tendency towards concupiscence. According to the so-called Jansenistic principles of truth and sincerity, it is not the external pious exercises that are important. What are supremely important are the inner intentions. No novelties are to be propagated. For a sound spirituality, all one has to do is to return to the authentic sources: to the Bible and the spiritual writings of the Fathers. Again, the most important characteristic is to nourish one's personal and inner devotion in harmony with the public celebrations of the church: the Mass, the other sacraments and the official prayers of the church, for example the Breviary.

Characteristic of this kind of spirituality is a Mass-book in which the Latin text of the Mass is found alongside a Dutch translation. The ideal was that the parishioners could follow what was said by the priest who was officiating before the altar. Presumably, the priest used to say the Latin prayers audibly, so that the congregation could follow him in their books. Other elements of this Mass-book are also interesting and important. Every Sunday and Festival has its own short historical introduction and a pious explanation. All the Epistles and Gospels are accompanied by a *florilegium*: i.e. by citations and quotations from the Church Fathers. As to individual spirituality, everybody who prayed for himself or for herself was spiritually nourished and fed by the common, genuine tradition. This particular life-style was distinguished, sober and austere.

In the Old Catholic congregations in the Netherlands, later customs such as the use of the rosary, the adoration of the Sacred Heart and most other late baroque devotions were quite unknown. Even in later times, the nineteenth century Dutch Old Catholics retained the tradition of a spiritual life which is characterised by its soberness and austerity. They did not become acquainted with the typical, popular devotions of contemporary Roman Catholicism: an excessive devotion to the Holy Virgin; the adoration of relics; the veneration of the saints; and the pilgrimages and the cults which were propagated by certain of the religious orders. What was characteristic of the Old Catholic life-style was the typical spirituality of the secular priests and their parishes in the period of the immediate post-Tridentine restoration. It still remains after the great changes which took place at the beginning of the twentieth century as a result of the influence of the German and the Swiss Old Catholic movements. There was a period of liturgical renewal which was coupled with an attempt to find a new direction for the Christian life in the context of modern conditions.

The main characteristics of Dutch Old Catholic spirituality, however, still remain the same: namely an attempt to combine an emphasis upon personal responsibility resulting in a serious Christian life-style without falling into mystical excesses or religious fanaticism on the one hand, and participation in the public worship of the church in its classical forms of the Mass and Vespers on the other. Bible-reading is facilitated by the availability of Catholic translations in the language of one's people. One's understanding of the Bible is enriched by the catenae of quotations culled from the Fathers and the writings of the Jansenists of Port Royal. So, in spite of the powerful German influences after 1870, the Dutch Old Catholics still retained their old traditions, but this organic tradition was continually adapted and readapted.

During the last few decades following the Second World War, some elements have begun to emerge which are really new: notably the foundation of a fraternity whose aim is to foster the devotional life in accordance with strict rules. In accordance with a very old tradition dating from the beginning of the seventeenth century, it was called the Saint Willibrord fraternity. The first aim of the fraternity is the translation of the old Dutch spiritual tradition of the *devotio moderna* for modern times. It was also influenced by contact with Anglicans: hence the regular retreats which are now a recognized part of church life. Daily prayer according to a lay-breviary has also been restored, and regional bible-studies are also organized for its members. But there are no experiments with typically new spiritual techniques such as the introduction of the Zen methods of meditation into the Christian life. More recently, some priests and laypeople have founded a working-group for spiritual renewal in the church. Although they have been influenced by the charismatic movement, they are unwilling to organize themselves into a kind of fraternity. Instead, they aim to renew the spiritual life within the traditional parish structures. The former Rector of the St. Willibrord Society belongs to this charismatic group. They organize conferences on various issues connected with the charismatic renewal of the church. Another trend, especially amongst some of the young priests in Switzerland, is an openness towards the spirituality of the Orthodox Churches. This manifests itself particularly in the form of the adoration of icons, and the introduction of certain liturgical practices from the traditional worship of the Orthodox Churches into the Old Catholic liturgies, such as the Easter celebrations. It is really a pity that our dependence upon outside influences is so great:

for there is a wealth of spirituality in our own tradition. Surely it would be worthwhile to explore our own spiritual roots? Surely it would be better not to repeat the old-fashioned forms *ad infinitum*; but rather to restore or to find a place for genuine, traditional elements of spirituality; adapted, however, to the needs of the modern world? Just as the Roman Catholics are recovering the mystical traditions of the Carmelites (especially the mysticism of St. John of the Cross), so it is necessary for Old Catholics to return to their own spiritual roots in order to encourage spiritual renewal in our own days. This does not mean, however, that Old Catholics should seek now to restore the old forms of Jansenistic piety. What is needed now are new opportunities to discover a Christian life-style in the context of modern secular life: combined, naturally, with a common liturgical expression.

The Old Catholic movement in Germany and Switzerland is a by-product of the protests against the dogmas of papal infallibility and centralized jurisdiction. The movement was originally started by certain intellectuals: e.g. professors of theology supported by well-educated laypeople. They came from certain circles in the Roman Catholic Church which were pleading for an open stance in the church towards modern culture and science. Their inspiration was derived from theologians who had been influenced by the Enlightenment and Romanticism. It is a well-known historical fact that Professor Reusch, who later became a bishop in Germany, had been a student of the famous theologian Günther who was eventually condemned by the Pope. The great leader of the protest movement was J. J. Ignatius von Döllinger. His roots are to be found in the theology of the Catholic faculty of the University of Tübingen, especially J. A. Möhler and his disciples. These were the theologians who protested against the new dogmas relating to the papal office. They conceived that it was their duty to organize their protest movement strictly within the structures of the church. So they established a 'diocese' of their own. Their intention was to organize themselves into a 'provisional' church for as long as the ecclesiastical emergency should last and there was no room for them within the Roman Church. That was why they called their bishop the Bishop for the Old Catholics in Germany and Switzerland. It is also quite clear that their protest was not just against the doctrinal innovations of the First Vatican Council. What was ultimately at stake was the idea of the Church and all its many ecclesiological ramifications. So they tried to transform their idea of the church into a living, historical reality: i.e. as a kind of counter-church in the specific form of their newly-founded 'emergency-organization'. Here, it would develop into a rather long digression if we were to tell in full the story of what the Old Catholics actually wanted and what they eventually managed to achieve in a very short period of time. But briefly, it should at least be said that all the programmes developed by the Catholic reformers during the time of the Enlightenment and at the beginning of the nineteenth century inspired them to such an extent that they worked out their ideas in the form of liturgical texts, pastoral letters and prayer-books. They trimmed the Western Catholic liturgy of its Baroque exuberances. They tried to restore the ritual to its classical style and form. Laypeople were given a responsible role in the worship and in the business of the church at every level. When confronted with the rather difficult task of describing Old Catholic spirituality, one feels the need to probe more deeply into the historical origins of the Old Catholic Churches. Again, it is only possible to do this briefly.

It is my firm opinion that some words written by von Döllinger in the Preface to his *Der Papst und das Papstthum*(1870) are highly significant for the whole of the Old Catholic Movement and all the relevant theological, liturgical and spiritual issues of that time:

We are convinced that the Catholic Church should adopt neither an aggressive nor a defensive posture over against the principles of political, intellectual and religious freedom and personal responsibility, and certainly to the extent that principles such as these can be understood in a Christian sense: and even as the direct result of the creative power of both the Spirit and the letter of the Gospel; rather the Church should respond positively to these principles and also encourage the search for purer and nobler applications of them. We agree, moreover, with the view of those who believe that a substantial and radical reformation of the church is both necessary and unavoidable, however long it is going to be postponed.

It is clear that von Döllinger's programme of reform arises out of the situation which obtained at the beginning of the nineteenth century. As far as the liturgical and spiritual renewal is concerned, this was inspired by men such as Sailer and von Wessenberg. Their influence on the processes of liturgical renewal in the diocese of Constance was so great that a considerable number of parishes in that particular area eventually decided to join the Swiss Old Catholic Church. In the field of liturgical renewal we should note the following changes: first, the introduction of the vernacular; secondly the reformulation of certain classical liturgical texts in order to encourage greater understanding and in the light of certain educational developments. But the most spiritual elements of the Old Catholic movement are to be found in the early pastoral letters of the bishops. They chose as their themes such topics as the Christian conscience; the freedom of the children of God; the duties of the worshipping community. In these letters, we can find a considerable amount of openness towards personal responsibility; so, in the period between 1870 and 1880 the Lenten duties, confessions and such like were made optional. The social responsibilities of the believer are emphasized, but without any sign of clerical constraint. We can also find many exhortations to take part in the celebration of the liturgy, especially in the Eucharist which is now seen as a source of inspiration in one's daily work and public duties. Again, we can see a new combination of personal responsibility and liturgical inspiration. The Old Catholic position devolves upon the peculiar task and duty of every Christian in social and public life without recourse to any form of coercion from a Christian organization operating in the political or the social sphere. The ultimate aim of the movement is a spiritual commonwealth, which is inspired by one's own personal Christian conviction as it is nourished and fostered by the sacramental life of the church.

But there is even more to be said. For example, Bishop Herzog the first Old Catholic bishop in Switzerland, is best known for his efforts to promote the liturgical and spiritual life of those believers who joined the Old Catholic movement for political reasons. His most famous work is a prayer-book entitled *Gott ist die Liebe*, which he published with the intention of fostering Christian family life. In his Foreword, Herzog expressed the hope that his book would stimulate a form of family life based upon prayer. Following the best traditions,[1] he includes prayers for both morning and evening, devotions which could be used in times of personal need, together with short introductions and meditations for the regular Sunday celebrations and the sacraments. By opting for this particular approach, Herzog placed himself firmly within the established Dutch tradition. The use of biblical quotations and the language of the Old and New Testaments in his prayers and meditations is also striking. His basic principles are as follows: the language of worship ought to be understandable to all of the participants; the congregation should also be able to join the priest in prayer; and the availability of the

sacrament of Holy Communion every Sunday is strongly emphasized. Together with the Jansenists, he abhors exuberance in
public worship. This can be seen in a pastoral letter dating from
1894:

Nobody maintains that he (i.e. the Pope) is leading the world into a deeper
understanding of the truth of the Gospel with all his manifold dispensations,
or that he can thus guide people towards new ways of worshipping God. And
even if he does pontificate on the subject of divine adoration, then what he
(usually) deals with is the rosary, or with the so-called Third Order of St.
Francis or with indulgences or with strange latter day saints.

It is clear what kinds of devotion Herzog abhors, and the way in
which he strives to restore a healthy spirituality is also clear enough.
He follows the precedents which have already been cited: spirituality
should be biblical, sober, and transparent; above all, Christian
spirituality should be a genuine inspiration which leads to a committed Christian life. Just as in the sermons of Reusch, this particular
idea is abundantly evident in those of Herzog. Both employ a fixed
scheme; both explain biblical issues in such a way that they ultimately have an impact upon the personal decisions taken by the
believer in his or her daily life. Both the church and (supremely) the
Sunday celebrations afford the Christian believer respite from his or
her daily labours together with the necessary inspiration and grace to
fulfil one's social duties throughout the week. This spiritual ethos is
typical of the whole of the Old Catholic movement.

Whether he actually succeeded is a debatable point. Bishop Küry,
his second successor as bishop, once observed that there was more
freedom than Holy Spirit in the hearts and minds of many Old
Catholics. He condemned liberalism as a form of ecclesiastical non-
commitment. So we can now see a new movement amongst some of
the younger priests whose goal is the realization of the ideals expressed by Bishop Herzog in our own time. Together with some young
laypeople, they founded together the so-called Fraternity of St. John
the Baptist in the late 1960s. They are striving to deepen the spiritual
life of the church by restoring the common prayer. They are active in
the field of liturgical renewal. They publish forms of daily prayer
inspired by the classical Breviary, and they organize retreats during
which contemporary themes are discussed. Their approach reflects
the 'diaspora-situation' of many of the Swiss Old Catholics, especially in the urban areas. This group is rather small, but it is influential amongst those young priests who are engaged in liturgical re-

newal in their parishes. In Switzerland, there is also the Fraternity of St. Nicholas, whose aim is the ultimate restoration of ecclesial communion between the Old Catholics and the Orthodox Churches. It is not unlike the Fellowship of St. Alban and St. Sergius: its activities are more liturgical than academic.

These are all developments which are typical of the present situation in Switzerland. This leads us to the question as to whether there are also similar movements amongst the German Old Catholics. In Germany, it appears that many priests and laypeople are joining the Fraternity of St. Michael. This was originally a Protestant group which was striving to restore the prayer-discipline of Catholic monasticism and spirituality within the Lutheran Church. It resembles some of the Old Catholic fraternities. We should also refer to the introduction of Zen-inspired methods of meditation by Professor Christian Oeyen. This particular phenomenon should be mentioned, even though its influence still seems to be rather marginal. As can be seen in the Old Catholic Churches in Germany and Switzerland, the main emphasis in spirituality traditionally falls upon worship as *the* source of inspiration for one's daily life.

It is not too difficult now to see certain family resemblances between Dutch and 'German' spirituality. This is by no means surprising, because they both share (to a greater or lesser degree as the case may be) the same Catholic tradition, and both share the same context: modern Western society.

But there are unmistakable differences between the Dutch and the 'Germans' on the one hand, and the Old Catholics who are ultimately of Polish origin. Unfortunately, information about current trends in Polish Old Catholic spirituality is difficult to obtain, but it is clear that their spirituality is bound up with their national aspirations. Indeed, the Polish National Church originated in a conflict between Polish immigrants in the United States and their Irish bishops.[2] Their feelings of national independence in a context of ecclesiastical dependency ultimately drove them towards a breach with Rome. So their search for ecclesiastical autonomy brought them to a point when they decided to join the Old Catholic movement. In their characteristic form of the devotional life, they retain certain traditions which are typically Polish. Thus they cherish specific forms of devotion which are dear to Polish National Church members but which are not fostered by the other Old Catholics. The Poles have, for example, their own special devotions to the Reserved

Sacrament and their special devotions to the Holy Virgin. Both in the United States and in Poland, typical forms of popular religiosity can be observed, but the use of the rosary, statues of the Sacred Heart of Jesus and other forms of late Baroque spirituality are not usually in evidence. Reference should also be made to the Mariavites and their adoration of the presence of Christ in the Holy Bread and their special devotion to the Blessed Virgin Mary. Again, we can see a typical national style of spirituality combined with various social programmes. They are also very active in the fields of teaching and education, and even in the trade union movement. But the extent of their influence upon other styles of Old Catholic spirituality cannot be measured or assessed at the present moment. More research is necessary in this particular area.

It is clear now that in these rather concise descriptions of the various components of Old Catholic spirituality there are considerable differences between the typical traditions, but there are also certain common elements too. First, all the Old Catholic Churches emphasize a liturgical style which inspires every believer, and ensures individual participation in the corporate worship of the church. Secondly, with the possible exception of the Polish churches, the Old Catholics emphasize the need to return to the original traditions in order to find the resources which one needs in order to live a genuinely Christian life in the midst of this world. This was why the use of the bible was restored to the laity. It was also the reason for the process of liturgical renewal which returned to the original sources for guidance, and for the republication of the writings of the Fathers. There was no cheap devotion. Popular styles of spiritual exuberance were discouraged. Public duty and spiritual life required, above all, the spirit of simplicity and sincerity. And, in line with certain specific developments in modern culture, both personal and individual responsibility were emphasized in the context of one's spiritual and social life. A certain trend in the direction of individualism, which is always a real danger in Old Catholic spirituality, was corrected by exhortations to the faithful to participate in public worship. In the liturgy, their role was therefore not that of the passive spectator. They were all active members of the worshipping community. This was precisely the reason why the liturgies, the prayers and the sermons were translated in such a way that they were 'understanded of the people'. The axis of Christian life in society is, however, individual (i.e. unorganized). So Old Catholic spirituality does not have a direct impact upon social life. This takes place indirectly and not deliberately. Its impact is the result of the hidden presence of a relatively small number of practising Old Catholics whose public life-style has been influenced by their spirituality.

Here, it would seem that the Polish Churches are the exception to the general rule. Their social impact is greater: indeed it is a function of the specific combination of Christianity and nationality. This combination also functions as a kind of social 'cement': i.e. it holds together a certain group in society. In the other churches, however, the inner life is not immediately directed towards the outward action of the community as a whole. The social situation of the Old Catholics, most of whom live in a diaspora or in very small parishes, is the result of this attitude towards social life. In conclusion, it is quite remarkable how the main stream of Old Catholic spirituality seemingly reflects the situation of religion in modern society: namely, the privatization of religion, and its banishment from the centre of public life to its marginal existence in separate religious groups, with their own characteristic expressions and life-styles on the peripheries of society. In this new context, and in this specific sense, the prophetic words once written by von Döllinger have now been amply fulfilled.

(With thanks to my colleague the Revd. Dr. Peter Staples (Utrecht) who corrected the original manuscript and translated the German citations.)

NOTES

1. Note especially the family resemblance between Herzog's prayer-book and the famous family prayer-book of Sailer.
2. See above p. 97.

8

The Face of Old Catholicism: Old Catholic Parish Life

MARTIN PARMENTIER

The best sources of information for the life of the Old Catholic parishes in Europe are the various national Church magazines, and the year books published by the German and Swiss churches since 1891 and by the Polish Catholic Church since the war. Unfortunately, these sources are hardly anywhere found together in one collection. In this chapter we shall survey Old Catholic parish life by looking at church buildings and parishes in the Netherlands, Germany, Switzerland, Austria, Czechoslovakia, Yugoslavia, Poland, France, Italy and Sweden.

In the *Netherlands* the history of the churches as far as their buildings are concerned is as different from that of the churches in other countries as the history of the Dutch Old Catholic Church itself differs from that of the other national churches. At the time of the Reformation, some one hundred and fifty years before the schism between Rome and Utrecht, the Catholic congregations were all driven out of their church buildings and were at first heavily fined if they gathered for worship in private homes. After some time it became less difficult to establish fixed meeting-places, and halls in private houses were converted into real centres of worship – the so-called 'hidden churches' (*schuilkerken*). These would generally be dedicated to the same patron saint as the old church. Hence, a number of Old Catholic churches today still have the same patron saint as an old church nearby which is in Protestant use; and the same is true in the case of Roman Catholic parishes of that period.

Most hidden churches were built in the seventeenth century and first half of the eighteenth. In the nineteenth century, when the Dutch Reformed Church no longer had a privileged position, it became possible once again to build Catholic places of worship which looked like churches. At that time most Roman Catholic hidden churches were replaced by modern buildings, though one notable exception in

Amsterdam is now a museum, called 'Our Lord in the Attic' (*Onze Lieve Heer op Solder*). However, because the Old Catholic Church (known at that time, and officially still, as 'the Roman Catholic Church of the Old Episcopal Clergy') did not grow in numbers, it did not replace all its hidden churches until the upsurge of building activity which occurred in the first decades of the twentieth century. Only a few hidden churches now remain:

(1) Utrecht, St. Gertrude 1634: situated behind the neo-Romanesque cathedral which replaced it in 1914.
(2) Utrecht, St. Mary 1640: reconstructed in 1860.
(3) Gouda, St. John the Baptist 1630: reconstructed in 1863.
(4) Delft, St. Mary and St. Ursula 1743: replacing an earlier one.
(5) The Hague, St. James and St. Augustine 1722: a fine example of Baroque, replacing the seventeenth century attic church still in existence.
(6) Zaandam, St. Mary Magdalene 1695, formerly a barn: restored in 1974, together with the vicarage when this became the residence of the Bishop of Haarlem.
(7) Krommenie, St. Nicholas 1612, formerly a stable: this, the earliest Old Catholic church continually in use, is now in bad repair, and, with only a tiny congregation, its future looks bleak.

The fine hidden church in Rotterdam of St. Lawrence and St. Mary Magdalene, built in 1698 and reconstructed in 1791, was unfortunately burned to the ground during the German bombardment of that city in 1940.

Although few churches are now in their exact seventeenth or eighteenth century state, most interiors still have an antique appearance even though the church itself may have been rebuilt much later. This typically conservative trait in the Dutch Old Catholic character leads a visitor to believe himself to be in an eighteenth century atmosphere, although the building itself was perhaps erected in the present century. Beautiful Baroque altars, pulpits, communion rails and paintings are to be found in almost every church except for a few of recent date. Often these items originate from the hidden church which preceded the present building, or else from others which were closed and had no successor. During the eighteenth and nineteenth centuries many parishes were closed or amalgamated. Even so, most parishes of the Utrecht party were always in the west and middle parts of the present kingdom. This curious fact was probably caused by the self-conscious attitude of the parish priests in those regions, who had most contacts with the Utrecht chapter and stood firm in the difficult years between the deposition of Archbishop Codde (1700) and the election of Archbishop Steenoven (1723).

The history of the Old Catholic parishes and their buildings in all the other Old Catholic countries is very similar. What happened in Germany happened in Switzerland, Austria, Czechoslovakia and Yugoslavia, and is still happening in Poland today. The great movement against the dogma of Papal Infallibility caused priests and their parishes to secede from Rome, and immediately a quarrel would break out between 'Old' and 'New' Catholics about the building. Here the attitude of the secular state made all the difference. In some places, as for example Switzerland, Roman and Old Catholics would be ordered to share the building, or else to sell their share to the other party. Since, at least in the early days, Roman Catholics never wanted to share their building with Old Catholics, the latter usually obtained the ancient building if they were in the majority. Otherwise they would build a new church.

In *Germany* the situation was very different from place to place. At first some advantage was gained from Bismark's *Kulturkampf* against the Roman Catholic Church, and from then on the German Old Catholic Church, as a National Church, closely followed the national government. The same however went for other Old Catholic Churches, something scarcely avoidable in view of the truly federal character of the Union of Utrecht.

In 1874, Germany had seventy thousand Old Catholics; today there are about twenty-five thousand. This reduction in numbers has much to do with the political fate of Germany in this century, as well as with the enormous isolation of the Old Catholic parishes and their individual members in that large country. 'Diaspora' is a key word today, not only in Germany but indeed in all other Old Catholic countries. After World War II all parishes in the east were lost, and many church buildings and vicarages were destroyed by bombing. After a small loss in Upper Silesia after World War I, the following towns which once had a number of Old Catholic inhabitants became part of Poland: Beuthen (Bytom), Birkenau near Gleiwitz (Brzezinka), Breslau (Wroclaw) with its Alte Sandkirche, Fellhammer (Kuznice Swidnickie), Gleiwitz (Gliwice) and Gottesberg (Boguszów) St. Peter and St. Paul. The latter is the only Old Catholic church in former German areas which is now owned by the Polish Catholic Church, and is due to the fact that a sufficient number of parishioners had remained there until contact was established with the Polish Catholic Church. Boguszów is a mining village, and therefore most inhabitants were economically too important to be allowed to depart. There are also Hermsdorf (Sobiecin), Hindenburg (Zabrze), Hirschberg (Jelenia Góra) with its ancient St. Anne church which is now Orthodox, Oehringen (near Gleiwitz), Oppeln (Opole), Rothenbach (Gorce), Sagan (Zagań) with its church of the Holy Spirit, Schweidnitz (Świdnica) and Waldenburg (Walbrzych). Several of these cities now have Polish Catholic inhabitants but, apart from Boguszów, they make use of different churches, as the parishes concerned came under Polish Catholic jurisdiction some time after the war.

The expulsion of the 'Sudetendeutsche' from Czechoslovakia caused a growth in the number of German parishes, and even the foundation of new ones, notably Neugablonz near Kaufbeuren, a city named after the old Gablonz (Jablonec) which was also an Old Catholic centre of importance. Other new parishes are Hanover, Kassel, Rosenheim and Weidenberg. In the German Democratic Republic, an area which counted hardly any Old Catholics before World War II, several new centres were founded, the main ones being Berlin, Blankenberg, Leipzig and Dresden. Before the war the only Old Catholic centre was Weisswasser. These Old Catholics, who are few in number and have extreme difficulties as regards organisation, are more or less independent of Bonn but are assisted as much as is possible from there. The only Old Catholic centre in East Prussia was Königsberg, now Kaliningrad in Russia.

In Germany a number of churches were built specially for Old Catholic worship. Most of them do not serve large congregations and they are therefore modest in size. On the other hand, this very fact, common to most Old Catholic churches everywhere, gives them a homely atmosphere which larger churches lack. As the latter are nowadays hardly full no matter the denomination, since modern believers are less attracted to mass meetings for worship than was formerly the case, this feature of Old Catholic ecclesiastical architecture is attractive to other people besides Old Catholics. Architecturally, Old Catholic churches differ little from their Roman counterparts of the same date. Since no higher authority has decreed it, the congregation is itself left to introduce a new altar with the celebrant at the Eucharist facing the people or not. Opinions differ here: generally, it is harder to introduce such an altar if the church furniture belongs to an age unfamiliar with this way of celebration, especially the Baroque period.

The names given to a new building at its dedication are seldom those of saints. More often they refer to Christ – there are several Christ churches – or to some aspect of his life and work – St. Saviour, the Transfiguration etc. This is obviously an expression of the Christ-centred teaching of the Old Catholic Church. Only when existing dedications are kept if an older building is obtained, do other names occur. Sometimes they are of a saint, or a Church Father of particular importance; as, for instance, St. John, St. Cyprian or St. Willibrord. In Poland alone a great number of names connected with the Virgin Mary are given to new churches. This has to do with the individual character of the Polish Catholic Church, or rather with that of Polish (Roman) Catholic Christianity as a whole.

The first German Old Catholic church to be built stood in Simbach (1874), though unfortunately, this parish was lost soon afterwards. Then followed Hagen (1877), München (1884, sold after World War I), Hessloch (1890), Zell im Wiesental (1892), Witten (1892), Saarbrucken (reconstructed, 1893), Krefeld (1894), Passau (1895), Karlsruhe (1897), Kattowitz (1898), Wiesbaden (1900) and many others. After the destruction caused by the Second World War the old buildings were either rebuilt or replaced by others elsewhere. Sometimes parishes have been able to acquire old churches which were not used by any denomination, such as St. James' Chapel in Koblenz (1335). This was part of a large medieval house which was entirely destroyed and rebuilt in a simpler form, now serving as a municipal office. The Gothic chapel incorporated in this building was able to be restored, and its small size made it exactly right for the Old Catholic congregation which acquired its use in 1968. Another interesting example is in Coburg, where the St. Nicholas' Chapel (1473) was acquired for use by a newly-formed Old Catholic congregation in 1967. The chapel was in very bad repair, but was beautifully restored and has some fine medieval wall paintings.[1] In both these cases the chapel is owned and maintained by the city.

The largest Old Catholic congregation in Germany is in Mannheim, and this has also one of the most impressive buildings, namely the church in the eighteenth century palace. In Frankfurt a new church was built after the war which has been jointly used by Old Catholics and Episcopalians from the very beginning. In Saarbrucken the church was rebuilt by the city authorities and is now shared by Old Catholics and Russian Orthodox: on the one side of the building is the Old Catholic altar, and on the other side there is a splendid Russian iconostasis.

A unique case is Nordstrand, where we find the church of St. Theresa of Avila which was built by the Dutch who came to lay dykes around the threatened island after a disastrous flood in 1634. This caused the death of nearly eight thousand inhabitants and the loss of some five thousand acres of fertile land. The local duke then invited the Dutch States to send experts to undertake the task of laying dykes. Those Dutchmen who came were Catholics, and mostly belonging to one family. They made the condition that they should own the reclaimed land themselves, and to this the duke agreed. These new landowners had contacts with Jansenius and Port Royal, and they invited other Jansenists to share in the cost of their work. Several Dutch parishes also took part in the enterprise. This is the reason why the Utrecht Metropolitan Chapter still owns land on Nordstrand today, although now it is no more than one acre. Until the last war Nordstrand was a parish of the Dutch Old Catholic Church, and was manned by Dutch priests. Today there are hardly any Old Catholics left on the island, but it is the centre for the North German 'Diaspora', and it houses the priest who is an charge of the area. The church of St. Theresa has a number of seventeenth and eighteenth century books (mainly French Jansenist), as most Dutch parishes have or had.

The Church in *Switzerland* has proved to be very stable after the initial period of struggle. The motivation behind the organization of Old Catholic parishes in Switzerland started, as in Germany, from the events of 1870. But whereas in Germany the number of professors and other scholars was significant, – at one stage the entire Roman Catholic Faculty of Theology in Bonn became Old Catholic! – the Swiss Old Catholic movement was characterized by its politically liberal inspiration which initially went far in its desire for church reform. This political liberalism, still notable in the Swiss Church, has its roots in the history of the Swiss nation with its stress on local independence; and it leads to such curious features as an annual church meeting being supported by the majority of church members, while, at the same time, they do not attend the Sunday services.

One concentration of parishes is in the Fricktal, east of Basle. Here, most 'Christian Catholic' (the Swiss name for Old Catholic) congregations possess the ancient village church as at Magden, Möhlin and Rheinfelden: an indication that the majority of the village turned against the Pope. This is explained by the fact that this area belonged to Austria until 1801, and the Josephinist and Jansenist tendencies there paved the way for later Old Catholicism. A survey of the churches in this area to be found in the 1958 *Christkatolischer Hauskalender* reveals that the present churches generally stand on the remains of predecessors of medieval or even earlier date. Another concentration of Christian Catholic parishes is in the Aartal; and this contains a number of interesting churches. Especially noteworthy is the ancient monastic church of Schönenwerd which still possesses a complete cloister.[2] The situation in French Switzerland has always been more difficult. Since the German part of Switzerland is mainly Roman Catholic and the French part mainly Protestant, the Christian Catholics in the French-speaking areas formed a minority within a minority (a situation comparable to that of the Dutch Old Catholics), and it was found less easy to live the Old Catholic ideal openly. However, the Old Catholics in France, who are centred in Paris, more or less lean on the liturgical and other achievements of this part of the Old Catholic Church.

The history of the Church in *Austria* begins as the history of the Old Catholics in Austria-Hungary, that is in modern Austria, Czechoslovakia and Yugoslavia since there were no Old Catholic congregations in Hungary. Before World War I the accent in Austria-Hungary was on Bohemia and Moravia, for most church members lived there. In the new republic of Austria formed in 1919, there were only three congregations: Vienna, Ried and Graz, and three thousand five hundred members. By 1926 however, the number had grown to twenty-two thousand, and in the next decades several new parishes were organized, although Vienna is still the place where most Old Catholics live. Since Austria has no church tax the parish priests derive much of their stipends from burying the less active Roman Catholics when these die. This, however, sometimes leads to a conversion of the deceased's relations! The Austrian Church now has some twenty-five thousand members. Some of the church buildings are historically interesting, like St. Salvator in Vienna and the churches in St. Pölten and Linz. Others are of a more recent date. A drawing exists of a new buiilding planned for Klagenfurt, but this congregation now has the use of an ancient church.

The Church in *Czechoslovakia* was full of life before World War II, but since most of its members were German-speaking they were ousted from the country when the war was over. In the German *Altkatholisches Jahrbuch* of 1954 and of 1957, some very negative reports appeared about the total annihilation of Old Catholic life in Czechoslovakia. However, this picture is too dark. It is true that, owing to anti-German feeling in Czechoslovakia in the 1930s, the Old Catholics went through a difficult time which culminated in the expulsion of all German members together with all other Germans; but the Church was decimated, not killed. In Prague there had always been a Czech-speaking congregation, and there must have been sufficient Czech members in the other parishes, as all these places have signs of life. In Cervené Voda the church is not in use, but is still owned by the Old Catholics, and there are reputed to be some three thousand members now. All churches were built by the congregations themselves, sometimes with financial help from outside, especially from Holland. Among the churches formerly belonging to Old Catholics but apparently no longer used or owned by them are: Arnsdorf (Arnultovice) in Bohemia, Meistersdorf-Ulrichstal (1897), Blottendorf (1901), Schönlinde (Krásná Lípa) (1901), and Tetschen-Bodenbach (Decín-Podmokly), Christ Church (1934). There was a church in Brünn (Brno) built in 1901, but this does not appear in the Year-book of 1921. The Czech congregation of Prague first converted a former printer's shop into its Bethlehem Chapel in 1904; and then in 1908 also obtained the use of the chapel of St. Mary Magdalene. It now has an ancient Romanesque city church as well. Apart from the parishes with churches in the places already mentioned, there were buildings for worship in many other towns and villages before the last war.

Without paying a visit to the spot, it is as hard to get information about Old Catholics in *Yugoslavia* as about those in Czechoslovakia. Before World War I, there was no Old Catholic organization in what is now Yugoslavia. Then, in the new republic which was formed, a rapid development in Old Catholicism took place. The Year-book of 1925 suddenly mentions the number of one hundred thousand members of the Croatian Old Catholic Church, and the list of congregations grows until, in 1929, we find centres in Croatia, Slavonia, Dalmatia, Bosnia and Herzegovina. However, in the 1927 Year-book, we find only a handful of parishes in Slavonia, Serbia and Bosnia. Yet, in the same year, it is reported that the bishop has recently consecrated a church to St. Cyril and St. Methodius in Karlovac. After the 1929 Year-book the curtain falls. Other sources reveal that the war years were particularly ruinous for the Croatian Old Catholic Church, owing to the Germans and local Roman Catholics. Today, congregations are reputed to exist in Zagreb, Stenjevec, Saptinovci, Osijek, Maribor and Novi Sad.

When we come to the Old Catholic Church in *Poland* we meet a situation which is as complicated as it is interesting, since the political history of the country has had such a bearing on the fortunes of Old Catholicism there.[3] The first Old Catholics in Poland were the Mariavites, but their membership of the Union of Utrecht was no longer welcomed after they went their own way to too great an extent. Round about that time, the Polish National Catholic Church in America had begun to 'missionize' the mother country; and this is how the Polish Catholic Church came into existence. Its first priests were only allowed to work in areas where there were no Mariavites; which meant that they were limited to what was formerly Austrian territory. The original Polish Catholic parish was organized therefore in Cracow. Nevertheless, there were at the same time a few parishes in Poland which were under the jurisdiction of the Old Catholic bishop in Bonn. Among these was the parish in Kattowitz (Katowice), where the church had been built in 1898 and which was German until 1918. Some of the services were now held there in the Polish language. After 1936 nothing more is heard of this parish, but before that a number of other names appear under the Bonn jurisdiction. In 1926 we read that a Roman Catholic parish of six hundred members in Gostyn near Nikolai (Mikolów) and a Mariavite parish in Zgierz near Lodz with three thousand members have joined together with a parish of the Polish Catholic Church in Cracow (the second one in that city), bringing the total of Old Catholics in Poland under the Bonn jurisdiction to six thousand. In 1930 however, only two parishes are mentioned; but five years later three new names appear: two of them having their own church. These occur again in 1936, and then the curtain falls. Meanwhile, in the 1927 and 1928 Year-books, we find a list of Polish Catholic congregations which include several of those in existence today. The bishop then lived in Cracow (today he resides in Warsaw), and an average of three thousand members per parish is indicated, with some fifty thousand in all.

Today, the number given is still fifty thousand, while a similar number of 'sympathizers' is claimed. However, the list of actual parishes has changed very much. This is due to various factors: first, the church has grown, even though there are today several parishes which were founded in the 1930s; secondly, a number of parishes are said to have existed in the east of Poland, especially in Lvov (Lemberg), which is now Russia, and these must therefore have been founded after 1927; thirdly, about half the present Poland consists of areas which were German before World War II.

The Second World War left Poland with numerous dead, many ruins and much unoccupied land. Roman Catholic priests who came over to the Polish Catholic Church would often be sent to Silesia (where fugitives from east Poland had gone), or to other former German areas to hold open air meetings and to celebrate Masses in the vernacular – a custom at that time still unknown in the Roman Catholic Church. They would then organize a parish and claim some previous German church which was unused and possibly in ruins. The Polish state often looked benevolently upon such action against the powerful Roman Catholic Church, but several of these newly organized parishes were lost later on. Another concentration of Polish Catholic parishes appears to be in the east, around Lublin. This area belonged to Russia before World War I, and conflicts in the Roman Catholic Church seem to have been more likely there, owing to the independent and Orthodox-inclined mentality of its people.

The formula which works in Poland today, and which – *mutatis mutandis* – used to work in the German-speaking areas at the turn of the century, is that when a priest and his congregation disagree with their Roman Catholic bishop, they join the Polish Catholic jurisdiction. It also works the other way round. An interesting instance of this in recent years occurred at Boleslawiec, where the Bishop of Katowice wanted to send the local priest elsewhere and the congregation protested by occupying the church and vicarage. The priest did not return, so more than half the parish asked for a priest of the Polish Catholic jurisdiction. The Roman Catholic authorities then went to court, retrieved the church, and sent back as parish priest the man around whom the whole conflict had begun!

Because in Poland, all churches are owned by the Church as a whole and not by the local community, the Polish Catholic Church only owns ancient churches which were originally Protestant churches in the former German areas. Exceptions to this may be due to special circumstances, such as a disused Roman Catholic building in Poznan and another formerly used by the Orthodox in Warsaw. The 'throwing out' principle seems to work everywhere; and hence many new churches are built by Old Catholics in Poland today. One interesting example is that at Studzianki, a village south of Warsaw. At the end of the war, German and Russian pantzers shot at each other through this village; it was therefore rebuilt as Studzianki Pancerne. When the inhabitants asked for a church they were not given one by the Roman Catholics, as these thought the village too small. The villagers then asked the Polish Catholics who sent a priest, and he built them a new church.

Among old buildings belonging to the Polish Catholics of special interest are the fifteenth century church in Sczezin, the seventeenth century church in Poznan, and a wooden – formerly Uniate – church with old icons at Zolkiewka. Wroclaw in Breslau is particularly noteworthy. Once Breslau was a spearhead of German Old Catholicism, a congregation having been founded there as early as 1872. From 1873 the Old Catholics were granted hospitality in the Protestant church of St. Bernhardin, and in the following year the parish became officially recognized. In 1876, the Roman Catholic Corpus Christi church was assigned to the Old Catholics at their request, or rather, the Roman Catholics ceased to use the building when they were ordered to share it with the Old Catholics, the reason being that the Pope had forbidden such an association with the 'new heretics'. In 1918 the authorities decreed that the Old Catholics had to leave the Corpus Christi church, and gave them the Seminary church on the Sandstrasse on hire from then until the end of March 1948. By the latter date however, the Prussian State no longer had any authority in this area. and most German Old Catholics had left. Today, the former St. Bernhardin church houses an architectural museum, and the Corpus Christi church is used for religious worship once more. The church of 'Our Lady on the sand' lost its roof and furnishings in 1945, but is now restored. The Polish Catholic cathedral of the Wroclaw diocese is a former Lutheran church, dedicated to St. Mary Magdalene and dating from the fourteenth century.

The Old Catholics in *France* were joined to the Utrecht jurisdiction in 1893. They successively worshipped in many different places, until finally in 1972, the 'Centre St. Denis' was founded. After that, a missionary station was opened in Sarcelles to the north of Paris, and worship is held there regularly. There is also an Old Catholic congregation in Lyon which is served from French Switzerland.[4]

In *Italy* there is still a centre in Scandiano, near Reggio Emilia in the north, but not much news reaches the outside world from there. Another centre is in Minervino di Lecce, in Apulia. At the beginning of this century there were a number of congregations in Italy, some of whom built their own churches. Now, all contacts with the mainstream Old Catholicism are by way of the Swiss Church.

The youngest shoot on the Old Catholic stem is that of *Sweden*, which came into existence little more than ten years ago. Today there are congregations in Malmo, Stockholm and Angelholm. These latest Old Catholics differ from the older ones, in that they react, not against the Roman Catholic Church, but against the Swedish Lutheran Church which, as High Church partisans they find insufficiently Catholic.

This raises the question of Old Catholic identity. How does it feel to be an Old Catholic? It will be clear to the reader that this depends very much on the country where an Old Catholic lives; and even inside a country there will be notable differences of 'feeling Old Catholic'. In Holland, where the sense of being a minority church was always predominant, the awareness of being oppressed by both Catholic and Protestant made the Dutch Old Catholic Church a very introvert community. The 'hidden church' fostered a mentality which is only very slowly beginning to disappear. Only after the last war, a real ecumenical break-through in the whole of the Netherlands brought the Old Catholics out of their isolation. Yet the fact that the new buildings were recognizable as churches had already paved the way for a more public witness, and in large parishes like IJmuiden and Egmond, things felt different in any case. For this reason, 'emigrants' from these parishes often find it hard to integrate into a smaller one. Socially speaking, the Dutch Old Catholic Church has been called 'an amputated people's church' (*Volkskerk, Volkskirche*). This means that in principle all strata of society were represented in the congregations, however small they were. In fact, there was some specialization according to the location of the parish: fishermen in Egmond, blast-furnace workers in IJmuiden (all originating from Egmond), flower and fruit growers in Aalsmeer, vegetable growers in the parish of St. James, Utrecht. This characteristic is slowly disintegrating, as are most traditional patterns in our society, and although in principle all strata of society are represented, the church has, in fact, lost most of its working class members, with the exception perhaps of larger parishes like IJmuiden, Egmond and St. James' Utrecht.

In the German-speaking countries, the Old Catholic movement of 1870 and later, never became a broadly supported popular movement. In Germany especially, many members of the middle class who reacted against Vatican pressures became Old Catholics. In the beginning the German church was called a 'Professors' Church'. Now that this generation has died out, it is difficult to characterize membership. However, it is obvious that a good many members came to what is now Germany from Czechoslovakia, or from the former German east.

In Switzerland and Austria too, people became Old Catholics for various reasons. In Poland, we can see an Old Catholic Church still *in statu nascendi*. The difference from the German-speaking churches is that the reasons why a priest or a congregation change jurisdiction are less obviously theological, or at least less theologically expressed than when the wound of 1870 was still fresh. It is therefore probably true that the Polish church is once more 'an amputated people's church', but that individual members of the congregation will be less conscious of their Old Catholic identity than those in other countries. So the Polish church today parallels on the one hand the development in German-speaking areas after 1870 in that priests and parishes separate themselves from the Roman Communion and join the Old Catholic Communion, and on the other hand the development in Holland in the early eighteenth century in that most of the members of the congregation will adhere to a priest they trust and not delve too much into the theological niceties of papalism or conciliarity – especially since the present Pope is a Pole. There are, of course, a number of educated Old Catholics in the Polish Catholic Church, but much remains to be done to inform every church member in detail about Old Catholicism as such. Until recently, the tie with the United States of America and Bishop Hodur was stressed more than wider fellowship of the Union of Utrecht. In the last few years however, the Polish Catholic Church has reflected more the Polish trend in Old Catholicism. Yet it is not strange that theological reflection comes after the actual development of the church, since theology always lags behind the facts. For the time being, the organization of the church, and especially the building of many new churches, has first priority.

Old Catholicism has always had an enormous interest in theology. The reasons are clear: a minority church in difficult, often hostile, surroundings, needs to reflect thoroughly on its identity. In 1725, a

Seminary was founded in Amersfoort which lasted for nearly two hundred and fifty years. Its modern buildings, which date from 1957, are now occupied by the National Council of Churches in the Netherlands, and the education of young theologians takes place in the University of Utrecht, in co-operation with Dutch Reformed, Baptists, Free Evangelicals and Roman Catholics, though for certain subjects – liturgy, church history and dogmatics – there are Old Catholic lecturers.

In *Bonn*, there is an Old Catholic Institute incorporated into the University. Here too, the students attend some lectures in either the Protestant or the Roman Catholic faculty, while the one Old Catholic Professor teaches dogmatics and other appropriate subjects.

In *Berne*, the Christian Catholics have a faculty of their own. There are Professors in church history, liturgy, dogmatics and New Testament. The remaining subjects are covered in lectures of other faculties.

In *Warsaw*, the Polish Catholic Church co-operates in the Christian Theological Academy, in which all the non-Roman Catholic Churches are represented. These are, apart from the Polish Catholics, Lutherans, Orthodox, Methodists, Baptists, United Evangelicals, Reformed, Mariavites (only students) and Seventh Day Adventists. Old Catholics lecture to all students in philosophy, sociology, Latin, psychology, logic and methodology, and to their own students only in Old and New Testament, moral theology and pastoral theology.

In *Prague*, there is a lecturer in Old Catholic theology.

Students from other Old Catholic countries generally go to Berne, or sometimes to Bonn. In Berne, there are always a number of Orthodox students, and several former pupils from there now hold teaching posts in the Orthodox Church. In principle, foreign students can come and study at all four institutes of theology, though only Berne has the right to confer the doctor's hood. In Utrecht and in Warsaw, this can happen only in co-operation with the whole faculty. In Bonn, one may write a *Doktorarbeit*, but not a *Habilitationsschrift*.[5] It is, however, always possible to come and study theology at any one of these institutes, and in certain cases, some financial assistance is available. But in order for one's study to be a success, it is essential to have at least a working knowledge of the language of instruction – Dutch, German or Polish – before joining.

While many of the Old Catholic clergy do their training in preparation for ordination in these institutes, there are some who are 'converts' from other Churches. Particularly in Germany and in Poland, a good many parish priests come over from the Roman Catholic Church.[6] Sometimes, a minister of another denomination applies to become an Old Catholic priest. As a rule, some instruction in the 'new' faith will then be required before he is allowed to officiate, and in the case of a Protestant minister he will need to be ordained.

Old Catholic priests generally look like their Roman Catholic colleagues as regards dress. In Holland, a clerical collar was adopted by Old Catholics when it became the Roman Catholic custom to wear it. When the latter abandoned it, most Old Catholic priests followed this example, with some notable exceptions, however, among the younger generation. In Germany, the Roman outfit of a white pointed collar over a black shirt has been accepted by Old Catholics. In Poland, American clerical collars are worn – Polish ones are hard to obtain – and cassocks if it is possible. Both Roman Catholic and Old Catholic priests in Poland generally go about in cassocks, although sometimes they are seen in a clerical suit and collar.

Contacts between Old Catholics and Anglicans on the continent are not all that they might be, owing on the one hand to the appointment system of the Intercontinental Church Society, and on the other to the establishment of the Anglican Diocese in Europe, the news of which was received with much disappointment on the Old Catholic side. But times have changed since 1910, when the Church of England protested against the appointment of Bishop A. H. Mathew on the grounds that there was a Catholic Church in England already.[7] Fortunately for both Communions, the Mathew enterprise very soon lost official Old Catholic support, though not before there had been repeated objections from England; and the events of 1931 marked the beginning of a much happier relationship.

So, after fifty years, we may ask: 'Where do we go from here?' The intercommunion/full communion between Old Catholics and Anglicans is no longer the unique thing it was in 1931: the growth of the ecumenical movement has widened the fellowship of both our Churches. Much will depend on whether Anglicans and Old Catholics remain separate Communions, or whether they each locally join others. If the various Churches in England come to a real unity, Old

Catholic-Anglican full communion will have to be redefined, even though Anglican churches in other countries may remain independent. If the Old Catholics reach a real agreement with the Eastern Orthodox – and this is theologically possible when political circumstances allow – the latter will certainly ask the former to redefine or review their relationship with the Anglicans. Already, the relationship between the Polish National Catholic Church and the Episcopal Church in America calls for clarification. Clearly, the future is full of uncertainties.

In the next decades it will become increasingly difficult for some of the smaller national Old Catholic churches to survive. Much will depend on the material resources, and, not least, on the participation and, it is to be hoped, the growth of the faithful. A shortage of priests, much more than a lack of finance, has forever plagued the Old Catholic churches, from the early eighteenth century, and then again from the 1870s until today. While there are numerous Roman Catholic clergy who wish to leave their church, it takes time to soak someone in the Old Catholic ideal: for Ultramontanism is deeply rooted.

The best thing for all Christians is that we should be together, as our Lord, according to the Gospel of St. John chapter 17, desired us to be. While therefore, our ideal on the short term basis may be 'independent from Rome and yet Catholic', what we really want is that all should be one and the church really and truly Catholic.

NOTES

1. See below p. 151.
2. There is a photograph of the Schönenwerd cloister in the *Alt-Katholisches Jahrbuch* 1981, p. 17.
3. For further information on the Polish Catholic Church see ch. 4 above.
4. According to the *Alt-Katholisches Jahrbuch* 1981 (p. 49), it is hoped to open a new centre for worship in the very near future at Rouen.
5. The *Doktorarbeit* is the doctoral thesis; the *Habilitationsschrift* is a very substantial second piece of scholarly work, on the basis of which the right to teach at a University is conferred [*editor*].
6. It is interesting to note that the Mariavites still do not accept Roman Catholic priests, though the Polish Catholic Church does.
7. On Bishop Mathew see p. 64 above.

9

Anglican and Old Catholic Theology Compared

J. ROBERT WRIGHT

Any attempt to compare Anglican and Old Catholic theology must be both selective, because of limitations of space even when documentation is kept to a minimum, and also subjective, because of differing views as to what doctrine or theology has been or is official or even representative of the two churches at various times and places in the past and present. This essay will seek to expose the early historical roots for such a comparison, then offer a few systematic observations, and conclude with some remarks for the present and future. The author's perspective is Anglican and American.

Historical Roots

The basic historical roots for a comparison of Anglican and Old Catholic theology go back to the Reunion Conferences held at Bonn in 1874 and 1875. Convoked by Old Catholic leaders specifically for the purpose of promoting reunion, these were informal and unofficial conferences of theologians from various churches but primarily Anglican and Old Catholic. I believe their points of agreement would still be widely accepted as representative of Anglican teaching today and they are frequently cited with apparent approval by Dr. Urs Küry in the doctrinal section of his standard work *Die Alt-katholische Kirche: ihre Geschichte, ihre Lehre, ihr Anliegen.*[1] These are the Bonn theses of 1874:

(1) We agree that the apocryphal or deutero-canonical books of the Old Testament are not of the same canonicity as the books in the Hebrew canon.

(2) We agree that no translation of the Holy Scriptures can claim an authority superior to that of the original text.

(3) We agree that the reading of Holy Scripture in the vulgar tongue cannot lawfully be forbidden.

(4) We agree that, in general, it is more fitting, and in accordance with the spirit of the Church, that the Liturgy should be in the tongue understood by the people.

(5) We agree that faith working by love, not faith without love, is the means and condition of man's justification before God.

(6) Salvation cannot be merited by 'Merit of condignity', because there is no proportion between the infinite worth of the salvation promised by God and the finite worth of man's works.

(7) We agree that the doctrine of 'works of supererogation', and of a 'treasury of the merits of the saints' – *i.e.*, that the overflowing merits of the saints can be transferred to others, either by the rulers of the Church or by the authors of the good works themselves – is untenable.

(8) (*a*) We acknowledge that the number of the sacraments was first fixed at seven, in the twelfth century, and was then received into the general teaching of the Church, not as a tradition coming down from the Apostles or from the earliest times, but as the result of theological speculation.

(*b*) Catholic theologians (*e.g.*, Bellarmine) acknowledge, and we acknowledge with them, that Baptism and the Eucharist are 'principalia, praecipua, eximia salutis nostrae sacramenta'.

(9) (*a*) The Holy Scriptures being recognized as the primary rule of faith, we agree that the genuine tradition (*i.e.*, the unbroken transmission, partly oral, partly in writing, of the doctrine delivered by Christ and the Apostles) is an authoritative source of teaching for all successive generations of Christians. This tradition is partly to be found in the consensus of the great ecclesiastical bodies standing in historical continuity with the primitive Church, partly to be gathered by scientific method from the written documents of all centuries.

(*b*) We acknowledge that the Church of England, and the churches derived through her, have maintained unbroken the episcopal succession.

(10) We reject the new Roman doctrine of the Immaculate Conception of the Blessed Virgin Mary, as being contrary to the tradition of the first thirteen centuries, according to which Christ alone was conceived without sin.

(11) We agree that the practice of confession of sins before the congregation or a priest, with the exercise of the power of the keys, has come down to us from the Primitive Church, and, purged from abuses and freed from constraint, should be preserved in the Church.

(12) 'Indulgences' can only refer to penalties actually imposed by the Church herself.

(13) We agree that the commemoration of the faithful departed – *i.e.*, a calling down of an outpouring of Christ's grace for them – has come down to us from the Primitive Church, and should be preserved in the Church.

(14) The Eucharistic celebration in the Church is not a continuous repetition or renewal of the propitiatory sacrifice offered once for ever by Christ upon the cross; but its sacrificial character consists in this; that it is the permanent memorial of it, and a representation and presentation (*Vergegenwärtigung*) on earth of the one oblation of Christ for the salvation of

redeemed mankind, which according to Hebrews 9. 11, 12 is continuously presented in heaven by Christ, Who now appears in the presence of God for us (Heb. 9. 24). While this is the character of the Eucharist in reference to the sacrifice of Christ, it is also a sacred feast, wherein the faithful, receiving the Body and Blood of our Lord, have communion one with another (1 Cor. 10. 17).[2]

The 1874 Bonn conference also adopted a statement opposing the insertion of the *Filioque* clause into the Niceno-Constantinopolitan Creed: 'We agree that the way in which the Filioque was inserted into the Nicene Creed was illegal, and that, with a view to future peace and unity, it is much to be desired that the whole Church should set itself seriously to consider whether the Creed could possibly be restored to its primitive form, without sacrifice of any true doctrine which is expressed in the present Western form.'[3] This position was agreed unanimously by both Old Catholic and Anglican delegations in 1874, and indeed (in an expanded declaration of six points) was the only subject of formal discussion and agreement at the second Bonn conference of 1875. Opposition to the *Filioque* is much less unanimous among Anglicans than among Old Catholics and it is included still in most Anglican liturgical texts of the creed, although in recent years the official Anglican position seems to be moving closer to that of the Old Catholics (and, of course, of the Orthodox) in favouring its removal.

From the Anglican side and at a more official level, the second Lambeth Conference, meeting in 1878 and attempting to formulate some response to the first Vatican Council of 1870 and its aftermath, outlined the first principles for an Anglican ecumenical position that would be in doctrinal agreement with the Old Catholics and others in Europe who had 'renounced their allegiance to the Church of Rome, and who are desirous of forming some connection with the Anglican Church, either English or American':

The principles on which the Church of England has reformed itself are well known. We proclaim the sufficiency and supremacy of the Holy Scriptures as the ultimate rule of faith and commend to our people the diligent study of the same. We confess our faith in the words of the ancient Catholic creeds. We retain the Apostolic order of Bishops, Priests, and Deacons. We assert the just liberties of particular or national Churches. We provide our people, in their own tongue, with a Book of Common Prayer and Offices for the administration of the Sacraments, in accordance with the best and most ancient types of Christian faith and worship. These documents are before the world, and can be known and read of all men. We gladly welcome every effort for reform

upon the model of the Primitive Church. We do not demand a rigid uni-
formity; we deprecate needless divisions; but to those who are drawn to us in
the endeavour to free themselves from the yoke of error and superstition we
are ready to offer all help, and such privileges as may be acceptable to them
and are consistent with the maintenance of our own principles as enunciated
in our formularies.[4]

Next in chronological order for a comparison of Anglican and Old
Catholic theology is the Declaration of Utrecht, 1889, which is the
official doctrinal basis to which all Old Catholic churches subscribe.
Resolution 35 (c) of the Lambeth Conference of 1930 affirmed that
'there is nothing in the Declaration of Utrecht inconsistent with the
teaching of the Church of England' and an English translation of this
declaration was printed in the official report of the 1930 Lambeth
Conference:

1. We adhere faithfully to the Rule of Faith laid down by St. Vincent of
Lérins in these terms; 'Id teneamus, quod ubique, quod semper, quod ab
omnibus creditum est; hoc est et enim vere proprieque catholicum.' For this
reason we perservere in professing the faith of the primitive Church, as
formulated in the œcumenic symbols and specified precisely by the unanimously accepted decision of the Œcumenical Councils held in the undivided
Church of the first thousand years.
2. We therefore reject the decrees of the so-called Council of the Vatican,
which were promulgated 18 July 1870, concerning the infallibility and the
universal Episcopate of the Bishop of Rome – decrees which are in contradiction with the faith of the ancient Church, and which destroy its ancient
canonical constitution by attributing to the Pope the plenitude of ecclesiastical powers over all Dioceses and over all the faithful. By denial of his
primatial jurisdiction we do not wish to deny the historic primacy which
several Œcumenical Councils and the Fathers of the ancient Church have
attributed to the Bishop of Rome by recognizing him as the *Primus inter
pares*.
3. We also reject the dogma of the Immaculate Conception promulgated
by Pius IX in 1854 in defiance of the Holy Scriptures and in contradiction to
the tradition of the first centuries.
4. As for other Encyclicals published by the Bishops of Rome in recent
times – for example, the Bulls *Unigenitus* and *Auctorem fidei*, and the
Syllabus of 1864 – we reject them on all such points as are in contradiction
with the doctrine of the primitive Church, and we do not recognize them as
binding on the consciences of the faithful. We also renew the ancient protests
of the Catholic Church of Holland against the errors of the Roman Curia,
and against its attacks upon the rights of national Churches.
5. We refuse to accept the decrees of the Council of Trent in matters of

discipline, and as for the dogmatic decisions of that Council we accept them only so far as they are in harmony with the teaching of the primitive Church.

6. Considering that the Holy Eucharist has always been the true central point of Catholic worship, we consider it our duty to declare that we maintain with perfect fidelity the ancient Catholic doctrine concerning the Sacrament of the Altar, by believing that we receive the Body and the Blood of our Saviour Jesus Christ under the species of bread and wine. The Eucharistic celebration in the Church is neither a continual repetition nor a renewal of the expiatory sacrifice which Jesus offered once for all upon the Cross; but it is a sacrifice because it is the perpetual commemoration of the sacrifice offered upon the Cross, and it is the act by which we represent upon earth and appropriate to ourselves the one offering which Jesus Christ makes in Heaven, according to the Epistle to the Hebrews ix. 11, 12, for the salvation of redeemed humanity, by appearing for us in the presence of God (Heb. ix. 24). The character of the Holy Eucharist being thus understood, it is, at the same time, a sacrificial feast, by means of which the faithful, in receiving the Body and Blood of our Saviour, enter into communion with one another (1 Cor. x. 17).

7. We hope that Catholic theologians, in maintaining the faith of the undivided Church, will succeed in establishing an agreement upon questions which have been controverted ever since the divisions which have arisen between the Churches. We exhort the priests under our jurisdiction to teach both by preaching and by the instruction of the young, especially the essential Christian truths professed by all the Christian confessions, to avoid, in discussing controverted doctrines, any violation of truth or charity, and in word and deed to set an example to the members of our Churches in accordance with the spirit of Jesus Christ our Saviour.

8. By maintaining and professing faithfully the doctrine of Jesus Christ, by refusing to admit those errors which by the fault of men have crept into the Catholic Church, by laying aside the abuses in ecclesiastical matters, together with the worldly tendencies of the hierarchy, we believe that we shall be able to combat efficaciously the great evils of our day, which are unbelief and indifference in matters of religion.[5]

In 1925 the Old Catholic Church of Holland declared its acceptance of the validity of Anglican Orders, which was endorsed later in the same year by the Conference of all the Old Catholic Bishops: 'We believe that the Church of England has wished always to maintain the episcopal rule of the Church of antiquity, and that the Edwardine formula of consecration must be accounted valid. We therefore declare, without reservation, that the Apostolic Succession has not been broken in the Church of England.' Apparently on the basis of this declaration Archbishop Kenninck of Utrecht explained at the time of the 1930 Lambeth Conference that the Old Catholic Church also regarded Anglican Baptism, Confirmation, and Eucharist as valid.[6] Anglicans had already been extended the privilege of communion at some Old Catholic altars as early as the late nineteenth century, and a similar privilege had been extended informally to Old Catholics by the third Lambeth Conference of 1888. Thus a considerable body of theological agreement, official, semi-official, and informal, already bound Anglicans and Old Catholics together in many ways prior to the Bonn Agreement of 1931. Much of it existed in written form.

The well-known theological agreement written by Anglican and Old Catholic representatives at Bonn on 2 July 1931 needs to be repeated here only for the sake of record:

1. Each Communion recognizes the catholicity and independence of the other and maintains its own.
2. Each Communion agrees to admit members of the other Communion to participate in the Sacraments.
3. Intercommunion does not require from either Communion the acceptance of all doctrinal opinion, sacramental devotion, or liturgical practice characteristic of the other, but implies that each believes the other to hold all the essentials of the Christian faith.[7]

The Anglican chairman of the commission, Bishop Headlam of Gloucester, wrote a letter of commentary at the time that noted, among other things, the absence of any doctrinal statements within the text of the agreement itself:

It was pointed out how undesirable it would be that we should attempt in any way to make a new creed, and therefore any statements of doctrine contained in it were omitted. It was suggested by the Old Catholics that we should begin by recognizing mutually the catholicity and independence of the two Churches. It was then decided that what was required on both sides was an admission to Sacraments in the two Churches. If that admission was granted, then admission to other ordinances would naturally follow. In order to removal all misconception, a statement was further added that nothing in this agreement implied that either Church would necessarily adopt the customs or habits of devotion of the other. It was felt that this statement was quite sufficient for our purpose.[8]

In spite of what Headlam reported about the suggestion of the Old Catholic members of the commission as to how they should begin, however, the first point of the Bonn Agreement (recognition of catholicity and independence) was omitted by the Episcopal Synod of the Old Catholic churches when they proceeded to establish intercommunion with the Anglican Communion on 7 September 1931. Points two and three were adopted in substantially the same form, but instead of point one the Old Catholic Episcopal Synod said only that it, 'on the basis of the recognition of the validity of Anglican Ordinations, agrees to intercommunion with the Anglican Communion.'[9] Whether this was seen as a significant difference at the time is uncertain.

Subsequently the three points of 2 July were approved by the convocations of the Church of England in 1932, ratified by the General Convention of the Episcopal Church in the USA in 1934 and 1940, and at various other times by various other synods of churches within the Anglican Communion, thus establishing intercommunion with the Old Catholics on a wide basis. The Bonn Agreement was extended to the Polish National Catholic Church in the USA by the Episcopal Church's General Convention in 1943 and 1946, and in the latter year was itself ratified by the Polish National Catholic Church in the USA. The 1948 Lambeth Conference in resolution 67 welcomed and subscribed to the Bonn Agreement and recommended it to other churches of the Anglican Communion, noting with satisfaction and approval the actions of the Episcopal Church and Polish National Catholic Church establishing 'full intercommunion' on the basis of it. The ninth Lambeth Conference in 1958 expressed a preference for the term 'full communion' (rather than 'intercommunion' or 'full intercommunion') to describe the Anglican relationship with the Old Catholic churches, and subsequent Anglican terminology has tended to follow this preference. It should be noted, though, that the Bonn Agreement of 2 July 1931 only states what 'intercommunion' is *not*, not what it is, and that even the Old Catholic formula of 7 September 1931 contains only (as point two) the limited statement that 'Intercommunion consists in the reciprocal admittance of the members of the two Communions to the Sacraments.'

Thus it may be said that at the highest and most official level of theological agreement between Anglicans and Old Catholics, very little was specified in detail. On an unofficial level, since the time of the Bonn Agreement many theological conferences have been held between representatives of the Church of England and the Old Catholic churches, and in 1980 and 1982 similar conferences were held but with a more broadly based Anglican representation officially appointed from many churches of the Anglican Communion. The issues discussed at these conferences reflect a wide range of theological agreement as well as points of divergence that will be discussed later below.

Systematic Comparison

If the foregoing is a chronological survey of the major historical documents that bind Anglicans and Old Catholics theologically, then it may next be in order to offer a few comparisons from a systematic point of view. Here a random selection of topics, and of observations within topics, will be made, and it will be assumed that the doctrinal section of Dr. Urs Küry's *Die Altkatholische Kirche* represents a 'normative' synthesis of Old Catholic theology and that the present writer is attempting to make a comparison to be taken as 'normative' by Anglican standards. Topics to be briefly considered include Revelation, Christology, Mariology, Veneration of Saints, Salvation, Sacramentology, and Spirituality.[10] Again there is much common ground.

For their understanding of *Revelation*, both Anglicans and Old Catholics appeal to the early church, primitive and undivided, but they do not regard it as the only source of divine truth. They both cite the rule of St. Vincent of Lérins (Utrecht 1889, no. 1), but they realize its limitations. They agree that Tradition may be used to interpret Scripture (Bonn 1874, no. 9), and in their acceptance of the *homoousios* and the Chalcedonian definition they agree that the church may use non-biblical language to explicate the biblical revelation. They generally accept the three traditional creeds, with less emphasis upon the Athanasian.

In *Christology*, they both emphasize the Chalcedonian formula, over against both Monophysitism and Nestorianism.[11] They regard the *Theotokos* doctrine of Mary 'the Mother of God', stated at the Third Ecumenical Council of Ephesus (431) and affirmed at the Fourth Ecumenical Council of Chalcedon (451) as primarily a Christological decision, and they emphasize that Mariology should not be totally separated from Christology. There is some divergence of opinion as to whether the Holy Spirit proceeds from the Father alone or from the Father and the Son, as noted above, but there seems to be some Anglican movement today towards the former view.

As for *Mariology*, which both Anglicans and Old Catholics believe should be closely related to Christology, they see affirmation of the Virgin Birth as an affirmation that God, and not just mankind, was active in the conception and birth of Jesus Christ, i.e. in the Incarnation. They agree, of course, that Mary can be venerated and can be called the bearer, or mother, of God or of our Lord. They concur in rejecting the dogmatic necessity of the doctrines of Mary's Immaculate Conception (Bonn 1874, no. 10; Utrecht 1889, no. 3) and bodily Assumption as constituting 'an inadmissible boundary violation, from the realm of the purely intellectual into that of actually accomplished salvation events'.[12]

In the *Veneration of Saints*, both Anglicans and Old Catholics see a union, a bond of prayer, between the church militant here on earth and the church triumphant in heaven. They would want to distinguish, however, between veneration or honour (*dulia*) given to the saints, and the worship or adoration (*latreia*) which is due to God alone. They would generally both agree, therefore, that God alone, and not the saints, answers our prayer. The veneration of saints, moreover, is not obligatory, but its most customary expression is to be found in public liturgical prayer. They deny any doctrine of a treasury of the saints' merits (Bonn 1874, no. 7).

Salvation, both churches generally agree, is not by any human work or merit, and 'faith working by love, not faith without love, is the means and condition of man's justification before God' (Bonn 1874, nos. 6 and 5). Dr. Küry makes a helpful distinction between the *revelation* of salvation and the *realization or unfolding* of salvation (*Heilsofhenbarung/Heilsverwirklichung*), and he raises a question whether confessional statements about the latter in the Western churches of the sixteenth century, such as the Anglican Thirty-Nine Articles of Religion, were really appropriate. Many Anglicans today, at least in the USA, would probably raise a similar question, but they might also think that some sort of modern Anglican 'confessional' statement, if one could be agreed upon, could serve the church to good advantage. There would be general agreement, though, with his assertion that salvation in the present is realized by both *word* and *sacrament*.[13] Anglicans and Old Catholics would also, generally, find no place for a doctrine of purgatory within God's plan of salvation. The Old Catholics allow prayers for the departed (Bonn 1874, no. 13), as would some but not all Anglicans.

In the area of *Sacramentology* there is a wide measure of agreement, especially since both are churches of a liturgical nature. A sacrament is defined in one Old Catholic catechism as 'ein sichtbares, von Gott eingesetztes Zeichen, das mit einer unsischtbaren Gnade verbunden ist'[14] and in this Anglicans recognize their own traditional catechism's statement that a sacrament is 'an outward and visible sign of an inward and spiritual grace'. There is also agreement that sacraments effect what they signify, and that they are means to the present realization of salvation. Baptism and Eucharist are the two principal sacraments (Bonn 1874, no. 8b). The Old Catholics, however, generally speak of seven sacraments (Bonn 1874, no 8a), but the English Prayer Book in Dr. Küry's view allows a thoroughly sacramental interpretation of the other five[15] and the catechism of the new American Prayer Book speaks of the five as 'other sacramental rites'. About Baptism both churches agree that it creates a permanent Christ-likeness and membership in the common priesthood of the faithful, but about Confirmation there is less of the same mind. The theology of Confirmation is at various stages of development in different parts of the Anglican Communion, whereas in the Old Catholic churches it would seem that Confirmation is still a necessary prerequisite for reception of communion and can be administered by a priest deputized by the bishop.[16]

The Eucharist occupies a prominent place in the worship of both churches and there is much theological agreement over it, some of which is summarized in Bonn 1874 no. 14 and Utrecht 1889 no. 6. The Eucharist is a perpetual commemoration, rather than a repetition or renewal. In it we receive Jesus' Body and Blood under the species of bread and wine, rather than in a crudely literal or merely figurative sense. Christ in heaven continually offers his once-for-all sacrifice for us, and in this Sacred Meal we enjoy communion with one another in the Lord's Body and Blood; neither church would say, however, that in the Eucharist we present the Body and Blood of Christ to God as an offering for our reconciliation or atonement.[17] Both churches stress the concepts of anamnesis, mystery, sacrament, sacred meal, and koinonia. Both churches have had to face questions over the concepts of real presence and sacrifice, the same two questions that figure so prominently in the 1971 Windsor Statement on Eucharistic Doctrine of the Anglican-Roman Catholic International Commission; almost as if anticipating the Windsor Agreement, Dr. Küry urges that the *fact* of Christ's real presence is what matters (the 'Dass') while the *manner* or *how* (the 'Wie') must be left open.[18] Old Catholics, and Anglicans increasingly, place an epiclesis of the Holy Spirit in the Eucharistic Prayer, but neither regards it as necessary to effect the consecration; for both churches, generally, it is the entire

Eucharistic Prayer that consecrates. Many in both churches would also see the priest at the altar in the Eucharist as acting 'in persona Christi '. Both emphasize the importance of the vernacular tongue (Bonn 1874, no. 4), communion in both kinds, and a congregation present and receiving, although Dr. Küry stresses that the Eucharist *can* be celebrated without any congregation present to receive.[19] Both churches permit reservation of the Blessed Sacrament for the sick, but they would agree that it should not become the object of a special cult in such a way that its true nature is obscured.

Both churches retain sacramental confession as optional and available (Bonn 1874, no. 11), but they deny that it should be obligatory and they disagree with the notions of the confessor as judge, penance as punishment, and the necessity of using an indicative form of absolution. Confession can also be general rather than private, and absolution can also be in petitionary form.[20] There is also some common sacramental understanding of marriage and of unction.[21]

As for sacramental ordination, in which the theology of both churches is also very similar, one again finds in Dr. Küry's Old Catholic treatment a number of points that appear in the 1973 Canterbury Statement on Ministry and Ordination of the Anglican-Roman Catholic International Commission. Thus, the Holy Spirit has arranged for many various offices and services or ministries in the early church, the threefold ministry of bishop and presbyter and deacon was a gradual development in the early church after the apostolic age, and ordination, which is for the sake of serving the entire church, is 'indelible' (Old Catholic) or 'unrepeatable' (Anglican).[22] The threefold service of Christ as prophet, priest, and king is shown in those who are ordained. Although there are three orders of ministry, there is only one sacrament of holy order. Both churches, it should be added, do not require clerical celibacy, and all orders of clergy are free to marry, even after ordination.

Finally, in the area of *Spirituality*, an important but vague and elusive term, there is a common (if not totally definable) theological ethos. The Old Catholic churches and the Anglican churches, in whatever countries they are found, are essentially national churches in full communion with one another but entirely independent and with no supreme or absolute authority over them all. From my own (admittedly limited) Anglican perspective, at least, the spiritual atmosphere of the Old Catholic churches seems definitely more

Anglican than Roman, even than post-Vatican II Roman, although such an impression would be difficult to state with any greater degree of precision. One might say, the theological approach we share is more rational and intellectual than it is mystical. It is more independent and free-thinking than it is tied to particular authoritative documents. It is respectful of tradition but reluctant to make binding decisions. And yet it is also closely bound to liturgical worship: *lex orandi lex credendi*.

The Present and Future

So much, then, for a brief, selective survey of some major points of Anglican and Old Catholic theology in systematic comparison. We turn, finally, to some remarks for the present and future and especially to two important questions that have been saved for the last: (1) the ordination of women and the authority of the Bonn Agreement, and (2) the primacy, jurisdiction, and infallibility of the Bishop of Rome.

As for the ordination of women, this is not the place to argue its pros and cons but rather to show how the effective authority of the Bonn Agreement has been questioned by it. Dr Küry says that women are excluded from priestly ordination, not because of feminine nature but because of 'the positive arrangement through the Apostle' ('der positiven Anordnung durch die Apostel'), and he does not elaborate beyond this.[23] The subject has been under Anglican discussion for a long time.[24] In January and April of 1976 the Intercommunion Commission in the USA met twice for official consultation between the Episcopal Church and the Polish National Catholic Church, which are the church bodies that represent the Anglican and Old Catholic communions in that country, and this commission (composed of bishops and other officially appointed representatives of both churches) in April issued the following statement in view of the impending crisis:

Since each Communion does not require acceptance of all doctrinal opinion or liturgical practice of the other Communion, should a Church of the Anglican Communion by its processes of legislation authorize the ordination of women to the diaconate, priesthood or episcopate and thereby hold a doctrinal opinion different from that of the Polish National Catholic Church, the Polish National Catholics would continue to support the objectives of the Agreement of Intercommunion, with the condition that ordained women would not be permitted in sanctuaries of the Polish National Catholic Church, nor to function in any sacramental acts involving its members or priests.[25]

Following the action of the Episcopal Church's General Convention in September 1976 authorizing the ordination of women, however, the Prime Bishop of the Polish National Catholic Church, who had himself been one of the signatories to the foregoing recommendation of the Intercommunion Commission, issued in November 1976 a statement terminating the relationship of sacramental inter-communion between the two churches until a determination would be made by the General Synod of the Polish Church.[26] In October 1978 that determination was made in the negative. Thus the agreement of the Intercommunion Commission was not sustained, in spite of the hopes of many in the Episcopal Church (then and now, including supporters of the ordination of women) that it would be.

Meanwhile at Vienna on 17 September 1976, the International Old Catholic Bishops Conference accepted the following declaration concerning the ordination of women (on the very day following the action of the Episcopal Church's General Convention):

The International Old Catholic Bishops Conference of the Union of Utrecht in accordance with the ancient undivided Church does not agree with the sacramental ordination of women to the catholic-apostolic ministry of deacon, presbyter and bishop.

The Lord of the Church, Jesus Christ, through the Holy Spirit called twelve men to be his Apostles, in order to perpetuate his work of the salvation of mankind.

The catholic churches of the East and West have called men only to the sacramental apostolic ministry.

The question of ordination of women touches the basic order and mystery of the Church.

The churches which have preserved continuity with the ancient undivided Church and its sacramental ministerial order should jointly discuss this question of sacramental ordination of women, being fully aware of eventual consequences relating from unilateral decisions.[27]

Of course there is diversity of opinion in both the Anglican and Old Catholic churches on the question of women's ordination. This was recognized in the agreed statement of the theological conference between Old Catholics and representatives of the Church of England at Chichester in April 1977: 'there is deep concern but at present no consensus within either of our churches nor between the churches in general on the issues either of theology or discipline involved'.[28]

Likewise, the eleventh Lambeth Conference of 1978 expressed concern for Old Catholic and other views on this question but also noted that 'the holding together of diversity within a unity of faith is part of the Anglican heritage'.

The present essay is not the place to enter a plea for any one theological position on this matter, but the events heretofore related do raise a question about the authority and effectiveness of the Bonn Agreement for facing such issues. One can readily agree that such 'a sacramental relationship carries implications which go much beyond that of simply receiving Holy Communion together' and that 'if full communion is to be fruitful, it is a desirable complement to have organs of consultation'.[29] Nonetheless, as has well been said, 'In the early part of 1976 both Polish National Catholics and Episcopalians earnestly sought to find a mutually-acceptable solution, but in the end they regretfully admitted their failure.'[30] It must therefore be admitted that the Bonn Agreement – with its absence of specific doctrinal statement, its failure to define for both churches what intercommunion (or full communion) really *is*, and its first point taken by Old Catholics in a form substantially different from that held by Anglicans – did not finally bear up in the American crisis of 1976–1978 even when there was an officially appointed Intercommunion Commission that held mutual consultations with good will on both sides. Can the Bonn Agreement, then, even with mutual consultation and good will, be ultimately effective without some theological principle of higher authority for its interpretation and implementation?[31]

The last question brings us to the final subject in this comparison of Anglican and Old Catholic theology, the possible place of the papacy in the church of the future. The classical Old Catholic (and Anglican) opposition to papal infallibility and primatial jurisdiction is stated in Utrecht 1889 no. 2. The first joint theological conference of Old Catholics with Anglicans from many parts of the world, meeting nearly a century later at Trier in April 1980, went on to say:

Both our Churches acknowledge that it is desirable to have some bishops who hold a special authority as *primus inter pares*. The Definitions of the First Vatican Council continue to raise serious difficulties for our Churches. Discussion of the issues raised by these Definitions needs to be carried on by our Churches together, especially taking account of the Declaration of the Old Catholic Bishops of 18 July, 1970, and the Venice Statement of the Anglican/Roman Catholic International Commission of 1976.[32]

Ecumenical theology moves on, though, and the Final Report of the Anglican-Roman Catholic International Commission, released in 1982, seeks to put the papal questions of universal primacy, divine right, ordinary and immediate jurisdiction, and even the concept of infallibility in a new light, so as to invite discussion on these matters from a fresh perspective. 'Authority', with special reference to this Final Report, was the subject of the next Anglican-Old Catholic Theological Conference, meeting at Vienna in September 1982, and a new question is now open to both Anglicans and Old Catholics: Can the recommendations of the ARCIC Final Report on papal authority be acceptable to them, even in solving major disputes about how to interpret and implement the Bonn Agreement?

NOTES

1. Urs Küry, *Die Altkatholische Kirche: ihre Geschichte, ihre Lehre, ihr Anliegen.*
2. C. B. Moss, *The Old Catholic Movement*, pp. 263–4, quoted from *Theodorus* (J. B. Mullinger), *The New Reformation*, pp. 255–66.
3. Moss, op. cit., pp. 262–3.
4. *A Communion of Communions: One Eucharistic Fellowship*, ed. J. Robert Wright (New York, 1979), p. 230.
5. *The Lambeth Conferences (1867–1948)* (London, 1948), pp. 170, 238–9.
6. Ibid., p. 237.
7. For background see Moss, op. cit., pp. 340–51.
8. As cited in the essay 'The Concordat Relationships' by William A. Norgren in *A Communion of Communions: One Eucharistic Fellowship*, ed. Wright, pp. 184–211, quoted from the *Report of the Meeting of the Commission of the Anglican Communion and the Old Catholic Churches held at Bonn on Thursday, July 2, 1931*, p. 10.
9. *Documents on Christian Unity. Third Series 1930–48*, ed. G. K. A. Bell, p. 61.
10. For my observations on Old Catholic theology, I am generally dependent upon Küry, op. cit., as follows: Revelation, pp. 126–36; Christology, pp. 137–60; Mariology, pp. 140, 155–7; Veneration of Saints, pp. 179–80; Salvation, pp. 127–8, 161–82; Sacramentology, pp. 180–219; Spirituality, *passim*.
11. The Chalcedonian definition of faith, as well as the Athanasian Creed, are printed in the new *Book of Common Prayer* of the Episcopal Church in the USA, p. 864.
12. Küry, op. cit., p. 156.

13. Ibid., pp. 127, 161–2, 180–2.
14. Ibid., p. 183.
15. Ibid., p. 216.
16. Ibid., pp. 187–90.
17. Ibid., p. 195.
18. Ibid., pp. 193–4; cf. Windsor Agreement, paragraph 6, note 1.
19. Küry, op. cit., p. 200.
20. Ibid., pp. 204–6. The new American Prayer Book in its services for 'The Reconciliation of a Penitent', provides for absolution *either* in the form 'I absolve you from all your sins' *or* in the form 'Our Lord Jesus Christ . . . absolve you through my ministry by the grace of the Holy Spirit.'
21. Küry, op. cit., pp. 207–9, 212–14. Anointing of the sick is provided in the new American Prayer Book.
22. Canterbury Statement, paragraphs 2 and 5, 6, and 7 and 15; Küry, op. cit., pp. 209–11.
23. Küry, op. cit., p. 211. For another, and much more extensive, Old Catholic view see Kurt Pursch, 'Frauen als Priester', *Internationale Kirchliche Zeitschrift (IKZ)* 63 (1973), pp. 129–67. Anglican literature on this subject is voluminous. For an example see R. A. Norris Jr., 'The Ordination of Women and the 'Maleness' of Christ', *Anglican Theological Review* Supplementary series no. 6 (1976), pp. 69–80.
24. Peter Day, 'Women's Ordination: The History of the Controversy Clarified', *Ecumenical Trends* (Graymoor, N.Y.) 6 (1977), pp. 26–8.
25. *Ecumenical Bulletin* (of the Episcopal Church) 18 (1976), pp. 27–8. The list of signatories is given, including three bishops of the Polish National Catholic Church and two of the Episcopal Church.
26. *God's Field* 22 (6 Nov. 1976).
27. *Ecumenical Bulletin* 21 (1977), p. 23.
28. *Ecumenical Bulletin* 27 (1978), p. 22.
29. Both are remarks of Bishop E. W. Kemp, the former in 'Bonn Agreement Jubilee Celebration,' *IKZ* 71 (1981), p. 226, and the latter in 'Intercommunion – Where Are We Now?,' *Saint Willibrord News* (Feb. 1981), p. 7.
30. Laurence Orzell, 'Background to the Polish National Catholic Church,' *Saint Willibrord News* (Ascensiontide, 1980), p. 18.
31. This issue of the *IKZ* for October-December 1981 (71:4) is devoted to thoughtful discussions of the effects and effectiveness of the Bonn Agreement.
32. Full text in *Anglican Theological Review* 63 (1981), pp. 72–3. The 1970 Declaration of the Old Catholic Bishops is published in *IKZ* 60 (1970), pp. 57–9, and translated in *Ecumenical Bulletin* 42 (1980), pp. 18–19. See further: E. W. Kemp, 'The Church of England and the Old Catholic Churches' in *Anglican initiatives in Christian Unity*, ed. E. G. W. Bill (1967).

10

Old Catholics and Ecumenism

GORDON HUELIN

Ecumenism is of particular significance for the Old Catholic Churches since, despite smallness as regards numbers, they see themselves as a bridge in bringing the separated churches together. Evidence of this outlook is clearly apparent in the proceedings of the International Old Catholic Congresses which are normally held in a different continental town at four-yearly intervals; and again in the volumes of the *Internationale Kirchliche Zeitschrift (IKZ)* published by the Theology Faculty of the University of Berne, 'a uniquely valuable storehouse of information about the ecumenical movement, especially in relation to matters of Faith and Order'.[1]

So, when the Ecumenical Movement began to blossom during the early decades of the twentieth century, Old Catholics were well prepared to seize the new opportunity offered and to enter into conversations with the Church of England, culminating in the Bonn Agreement of 1931, noteworthy as 'the one example in the West of intercommunion between a Church which passed through the crisis of the Reformation in the sixteenth century and another which, though in a sense it has had its own reformation, escaped the perturbations of that difficult time'.[2]

(a) The Anglican Communion

The Bonn Agreement was signed on 2 July 1931. A letter subsequently addressed by the Archbishop of Canterbury, Cosmo Lang, to the Archbishop of Utrecht, Francis Kenninck said:

I rejoice that the happy relations established by you and the other representatives of the Old Catholic Churches with the Bishops of the Anglican Communion at the Lambeth Conference have borne fruit so soon, that the Bishops of the Old Catholic Churches have so fully and generously endorsed the agreement reached by the Commission which met at Bonn in July, and that the way is now made plain for full intercommunion between our Churches.[3]

Four months later, he was able to state that both the Convocations of Canterbury and York had adopted the resolutions of the Bonn Agreement 'unanimously and with real enthusiasm'.[4]

The immediate consequences of this intercommunion were three-fold:

(1) It led to mutual participation in episcopal consecrations. The journey made to London by the Old Catholic Bishop of Haarlem, Mgr. Henry van Vlijmen, to take part in the consecration at St. Paul's Cathedral of George F. Graham-Brown as Bishop of the Church of England in Jerusalem, and of Bertram Simpson as Bishop of Kensington on 24 June 1932, marked the beginning of many journeys of this kind. The most recent was that made by Archbishop Kok of Utrecht in July 1977 when Ambrose Weekes was consecrated in the Royal Chapel at Greenwich to serve as a bishop in the diocese of Gibraltar and jurisdiction of Fulham.

In turn, Anglican bishops have shared in various Old Catholic consecrations, as for example, in June 1937, when the Bishops of Gloucester and Fulham participated in the act of consecration at St. Gertrude's Cathedral in Utrecht when Andreas Rinkel succeeded Francis Kenninck as Archbishop. This is enough to dispel the idea that the participation of Old Catholics in the consecration of Anglican bishops helps in any way to validate their orders. In fact, after receiving a letter in which such a suggestion was put forward, Dr. Rinkel wrote back: 'The meaning of this will not be to correct our consecrations, but is a testimony of our mutual recognized catholicity'; and again, 'The idea that this mutual partaking should mean a correction of the apostolic succession cannot be accepted'.[5]

(2) It brought about an exchange of visits. The earliest of these took place in September 1932, when Bishop Berends of Deventer headed a party of Old Catholics visiting England. The members spent several hours in Canterbury where they were shown round the cathedral by the dean and attended Evensong; next day they were welcomed by the Cowley Fathers at Oxford prior to sight-seeing; and on the Sunday they were present at the Eucharist in St. Paul's Cathedral.[6] It heralded those exchange visits which have resulted in lasting friendships, many of which have been arranged by the Society of St. Willibrord.

(3) It meant that Anglicans and Old Catholics were able to share in each other's sacraments. Thus, in the autumn of 1932, the Bishop of Fulham reported that a number of isolated English churchgoers on

the continent had received Holy Communion, who previously were unable to do so.[7] As far as Old Catholics in England were concerned, they could in future attend Anglican worship and would not therefore need the ministrations of their own clergy. It is important to bear this in mind, since it clearly shows that bishops in England who claim to be Old Catholics are, in reality *Episcopi vagantes*. Dr. Rinkel made this plain in a formal statement issued by him in October 1954:

I declare in the name of the whole Episcopacy of the Netherlands of the Old Catholic Church as well as the Chairman of the International Conference of Old Catholic Bishops united by the Declaration of Utrecht September 1889, that there are no Old Catholic clergy working independently or under our jurisdiction in England and that the only Church with which the Old Catholic Churches are in communion is the Church of England itself. I declare also that all people calling themselves in England to be Old Catholic priests or bishops are unknown to us and not in communion with the See of Utrecht or in any way under the jurisdiction of a member of the above mentioned International Conference. I declare also that the Old Catholic Churches do not acknowledge the ordination and consecration of such people calling themselves Old Catholic, but consider their ordinations and consecrations as invalid, null and void.[8]

No doubt the question will have arisen as to why the Anglican and American Episcopal Churches still maintain separate jurisdictions in parts of Europe where there are already Old Catholic churches. As the contributor of an article to the journal *Theology* bluntly put it: 'Should wealthy American or English congregations exist quite contentedly alongside small and struggling Old Catholic neighbours?'[9] The 1968 Lambeth Conference, in its sixty-third Resolution, deplored the existence of these parallel Anglican jurisdictions, and recommended that the Lambeth Consultative Body should give early attention to the problems involved. Yet this situation still remains as one of the major causes of the aloofness which one so frequently encounters between Anglicans and Old Catholics on the continent.

The period which followed the signing of the Bonn Agreement was marked by the growing determination of the Nazis in Germany, under the leadership of Adolf Hitler, to dominate Europe. Indeed Anglican representatives attending the International Old Catholic Congress held at Constance in 1934, must have regarded it as ominous that, at the opening session, the Deputy of the Culture Minister for Bonn gave the 'Heil Hitler' salute, and this was returned with vigour. When the Second World War broke out in September

1939, plans were already in hand to commemorate the twelve hundredth anniversary of St. Willibrord's death. The Archbishop of Utrecht who had accepted an invitation to preach at a special service in Westminster Abbey in November, felt bound to yield to the wishes of his cathedral Chapter that he should not leave Holland. However, in spite of preliminary hesitations, four Anglicans – the Bishops of Gloucester and Fulham, Canon J. A. Douglas and the Reverend Philip Usher – managed to reach Utrecht for a thanksgiving service in St. Gertrude's Cathedral on 6 November. At this service the Bishop of Gloucester preached a memorable sermon on St. Willibrord, ending with the words: 'It is a time of darkness and gloom. There have been many such in history. We sometimes trouble for the future. But we believe that if we as Christians have faith, the troubles will pass. Let it make us work more earnestly that the kingdom of this world may become the Kingdom of Christ. And that God's will may prevail in the world'.[10] On the following day the four Anglicans accompanied the Old Catholics to the Dom Cathedral for the national celebrations.

During the grim years ahead it was the Old Catholics who, on more than one occasion, demonstrated the reality of intercommunion. In Germany, although at the outbreak of war the Old Catholics were forbidden by Hitler to have any formal relations with Anglicans, they undertook the spiritual care of those who remained there. In Switzerland, following the fall of France, the Bishop of Berne, Adolf Küry, at the request of the Bishop of Fulham, confirmed Anglican candidates, and his action was much appreciated. In Java, a Dutch Old Catholic priest gave great help to English people during the Japanese occupation. In Holland, Old Catholics carefully hid the registers and plate belonging to the Anglican Church. Immediately the war was over, they granted the free use of their churches to Church of England army chaplains. At the Hague, where the English church had been destroyed by bombing, confirmation was administered in November 1945 by the Bishop of Dover in the eighteenth century 'hidden church' of St. Augustine belonging to Old Catholics, and the Bishop of Deventer expressed the gratitude of his church and nation to the British for all that the liberation meant to Holland.[11]

Now it was the turn of the Anglicans to give aid to the Old Catholics. In the spring of 1945, when it was obvious that Holland would soon be freed, Archbishop Geoffrey Fisher referred in a letter to the Chaplain General to his eager desire to 'establish relations with the Archbishop of Utrecht, Dr. Rinkel, and the other leaders of Dutch Old Catholics at the earliest possible moment' and 'to demonstrate how dear to us are the bonds of intercommunion between us and the Old Catholic Churches'.[12] It soon became evident how desperate the Dutch situation was. Everyone needed clothes, socks and shoes. Archbishop Rinkel himself urgently required new tyres for his car to enable him to carry on his work. He also requested bicycles for his clergy who, he said, had 'only their *pedes apostolorum*, nearly without boots!'[13] Several English parishes responded generously. The congregation of Mortlake in south London, supplied the archbishop with tyres; the people of All Saints' Chatham gave help to those in Arnhem; while others sent parcels. At St. Bartholomew's in Dublin a parcel was left by a small girl beside the Christmas tree, marked simply: 'For the children of Holland from Joan Maguire'.[14] All this so deeply moved the archbishop that he could only express astonishment that people who scarcely knew the Old Catholics had shown so much interest in them, and had given such evidence of love on their behalf.[15]

By 1947 conditions had sufficiently improved for Dr. Rinkel to accept the invitation to visit England. Accompanied by Professor B. A. van Kleef, he was the guest of the Archbishops of Canterbury, Wales and Dublin and the Primus of the Scottish Episcopal Church. It was on this occasion that he received from Geoffrey Fisher the Lambeth Cross, a decoration conferred by the Archbishop of Canterbury on representatives of other churches who had rendered exceptional service to the cause of Christian unity, particularly as regards the strengthening of the relations between their Churches and the Anglican Communion. Archbishop Rinkel was impressed by the warm reception given him in Dublin, and saw no reason why there should not be intercommunion between the Old Catholic Church and that of Ireland. Three years later, when the General Synod of the Church of Ireland accepted the Bonn Agreement, C. B. Moss, the doughty champion and historian of the Old Catholic Church, noted with delight that only one member of the House of Clergy out of more than a hundred had voted against, and that immediately afterwards he fell down in a fit and had to be carried out![16]

A Lambeth Conference; an International Old Catholic Congress at Hilversum; and the inauguration of the World Council of

Churches at Amsterdam: all these took place in 1948 with ecumenism at the heart of each. The Archbishop of Utrecht attended the opening of the Lambeth Conference, the members of which warmly welcomed the Bonn Agreement and noted the value of the precedent set by its terms for similar agreements with other independent Churches. At the International Old Catholic Congress both Bishop Adolf Küry of Berne and Archbishop Rinkel spoke on the ecumenical movement. The Congress ended with a rally at which the Anglican delegates were welcomed with enthusiasm, and the first performance was given by an augmented choir from Utrecht of an Oratorio *The Song of Unity*, specially written for the World Council of Churches' Assembly in Amsterdam by Bishop Lagerwey of Deventer, with music by Alex de Jong, Old Catholic organist at the Hague.[17]

The 1950s were years of renewal, as well as of the strengthening of existing links. In Germany, where the Old Catholic churches had suffered grievously during the War, there was under the leadership of Bishop Josef Demmel a remarkable growth which showed itself in the building of new churches, or in the sharing of others with Anglicans and Lutherans. The Old Catholics in Berlin celebrated the twenty-fifth anniversary of the Bonn Agreement with a Eucharist in the Danish church where they had enjoyed hospitality ever since the one they had previously used was destroyed by bombing. Greetings were brought from London by an Anglican priest, Ernest Gordon – himself a former refugee from Nazi Germany – who preached a sermon which was short by German standards! Members of the Lutheran, Moravian and Baptist Churches, and of the Salvation Army shared in the service and reception afterwards. For some of them it was their first experience of seeing the Old Catholic Church in action. How tragic that, only four years later, this parish should have been torn apart by the Berlin wall.[18] At a conference for Royal Air Force chaplains and German Old Catholic priests held at Cologne in 1958 the proposal was put forward that some Anglican ordinands might undertake part of their theological training at the seminary in Bonn. It was felt that the deepening of understanding between the two churches resulting from such an experiment would more than outweigh the practical difficulties and the expense involved. The old seminary in Bonn was replaced in 1961 by a modern residential building called the Döllinger Haus, part of which became an ecumenical centre where students belonging to the Anglican,

Roman Catholic, Orthodox and Reformed Churches were able to stay and study together. Its first director was Professor Werner Küppers who remained a devoted ecumenist until his death in 1980.

To mark the silver jubilee of the Bonn Agreement, C. B. Moss contributed an article for the *Church Times*, describing the circumstances in which that agreement was brought about and assessing its value.[19] Léon Gauthier, who later became Bishop in Berne, attempted a similar task from the Old Catholic viewpoint in the *IKZ*. He drew attention to the numerous benefits which the agreement had conferred on both Communions. At the same time he mentioned certain delicate questions which continued to pose problems. It was good therefore, that a conference between theologians of the two Churches – the first since the signing of the Bonn Agreement – was planned to take place immediately before the International Old Catholic Congress in the autumn of 1957.[20]

Both the Conference and Congress were held at Rheinfelden, a small town on the Swiss bank of the Rhine, where the beautiful twelfth century parish church of St. Martin belongs to the Old Catholics. At the Conference, Old Catholics and Anglicans of varying traditions read papers on the theology of the Eucharist, all of which demonstrated a remarkable unanimity of outlook. The theme of the Congress was that of the laity's role in the church and the world; and here Archbishop Rinkel emphasized the importance of ecumenism for Old Catholics, and the fact that whatever the difficulties, they must continue to participate in the World Council of Churches. After sharing in the final Eucharist with its congregation of at least a thousand, Kenneth Riches, the then Bishop of Lincoln, wrote: 'We came away with the impression of a new vigour stirring in the Old Catholic churches, notably amongst some of their young priests and theologians'.[21]

During the 1960s more of what Léon Gauthier had described as 'delicate questions' presented themselves. These were:

(1) The question as to whether the Church of England should enter into communion with the United Churches of North India and Pakistan. Certain members of both the Canterbury and York Convocations expressed the opinion that the Old Catholics should be consulted, because the Church of England relationship of full communion with them was at present unique. Some idea of the anxiety felt by Old Catholics can be gauged from Dr. Rinkel's letter to Bishop Scaife of the diocese of Western New York in which he said: 'I

don't suppose that our Churches will break away from the Anglican Communion; it is never good to break up what has been builded up with such great care, after many serious discussions and with much cautiousness, but I am afraid that it will give many difficulties in the future, at most in the Anglican Communion itself'.[22]

(2) The theological ferment which followed the publication of *Honest to God* by the Bishop of Woolwich, John Robinson. Both the book and its author were taken severely to task by Hans Frei of Berne at the 1965 International Old Catholic Congress held in Vienna. He rejected its assertions, and pronounced the incompatibility of such a theology with the faith of the old church. The purely decorative role which the bishop attributed to the Holy Spirit seemed to Frei a decisive reason for rejecting the book. He had no hesitation in qualifying Robinson's most daring theses, since they called in question the very substance of Christian dogma, namely the redemptive work of Christ.[23]

(3) The proposed scheme for Anglican-Methodist reunion which became a topic of major concern in English religious circles, and was the subject of numerous Reports. Once again, Old Catholics had reservations. Having discussed the scheme fully at a conference held at Bonn in April 1969, their bishops concluded that it was right to say 'Yes' to the ordinal, and not right to say 'No' absolutely to the scheme as a whole.[24] Dr. Michael Ramsey, a keen supporter of the scheme, expressed his thankfulness.[25]

Despite these difficulties the 1960s saw further progress in relations between Old Catholics and Anglicans. Among them was the ratification of the Bonn Agreement by the two churches of the Anglican Communion which had failed to take such action earlier. In August 1960, the Archbishop of Sydney wrote to the Archbishop of Utrecht confirming its ratification by the Church of England in Australia and Tasmania. Two years later, Michael Yashiro, Presiding Bishop of the Holy Catholic Church of Japan, explained that with the loss of all pre-war records it was impossible to find documents establishing a formal recognition of full communion between the Old Catholic Church and his own, but he had no doubt that such a relationship had long been taken for granted on the Japanese side.[26]

In 1961, prior to the International Old Catholic Congress at Haarlem, a theological conference was held at Amersfoort. Here Michael Ramsey, who was the first Archbishop of Canterbury to share in such a gathering, gave a paper on 'The Anglican understanding of the place of the Fathers in the life of the Church'. He specially drew attention to the way in which Anglicans, Old Catholics and Orthodox shared a common heritage. Later, he made three points:

(1) Anglicans and Old Catholics could rightly and usefully hold conversations with other Christians anywhere, provided that actual steps towards full communion with others were taken jointly;

(2) full communion should be expressed not only by contacts between leaders, but there should be increasing contacts between Anglicans and Old Catholics at all levels;

(3) the two Churches should share their spiritual heritage and assist each other as much as possible in the development of their spiritual life.

A criticism sometimes levelled against the Old Catholics is that they lack evangelistic zeal. It was therefore particularly pleasing that at the International Old Catholic Congress, a Dutch representative was able to report that for the past five years Old Catholics in Holland, and even more in Switzerland, had been supporting work in an Anglican diocese in South Africa. He urged members of the Congress to spread the news of this venture among their friends and to increase their moral and financial aid on behalf of this work.

When Archbishop Rinkel celebrated the silver jubilee of his consecration in June 1962, Dr. Stopford, the Bishop of London, attended a service in St. Gertrude's Cathedral, and presented gifts from the Archbishop of Canterbury and himself. In 1969 an unusual honour was conferred upon two Anglican priests, John Burley and John Satterthwaite, by their appointment as Honorary Canons of the cathedral of Utrecht. Both of them, the former as Dr. Rinkel's chaplain at three Lambeth Conferences, and the latter as Secretary of the Church of England Council on Foreign Relations, had rendered singular services to the Old Catholic Church. The contribution which Andreas Rinkel had made in fostering good relations between Old Catholics and Anglicans ever since the days when he had taken part in the discussions leading to the Bonn Agreement was immense. Now, because of poor health and advancing years, he needed someone to assist him in his episcopal duties. So, in December 1969, Marinus Kok, a professor of the seminary at Amersfoort, was consecrated in St. Gertrude's Cathedral as Bishop Coadjutor with the right of succession. Some six months later he became Archbishop of Utrecht.

The new archbishop's task in the 1970s proved far from easy.

'You know, just as I have known it for about five years, that the episcopal dignity is crowned with a crown of thorns' he wrote to Eric Kemp, on receiving news of the latter's appointment as Bishop of Chichester.[27] Certainly the fresh developments in ecumenical relationships posed problems and dangers. At the Berne International Old Catholic Bishops' Conference in 1972, further consideration was given to the proposed scheme of union between Anglicans and Methodists. From a letter which Archbishop Kok addressed to Michael Ramsey and other leading English churchmen, it was plain that Old Catholics were still uneasy about the scheme, and above all the possibility of a split in the Church of England which could place them in an embarassing situation in the future.[28] This crisis was avoided, since the scheme failed to gain the necessary majority of votes in the Anglican General Synod. Another difficulty faced the Archbishop of Utrecht at the Assembly of the Central Committee of the World Council of Churches in 1972, when he was asked to celebrate the Eucharist but declined on discovering that leaders of various Protestant Churches had been invited to concelebrate. Nor did it ease matters when he learned that an American bishop had taken his place without consulting him. 'Comprehensiveness is good', he said, 'but it can go too far when we do not maintain our opinions on the Catholicity and Apostolicity of the Church, the ministry and the sacraments.'[29] More recently, Old Catholics have been troubled by the growing readiness on the part of some Anglicans to promote the movement for the ordination of women. Marinus Kok had justifiably stressed the view that when two churches are in full communion with each other, there should be dialogue before crucial action of this kind is taken by either one. In an article which appeared in *The Times* a few days before the celebration of the fiftieth birthday of the Bonn Agreement, entitled 'The Utrecht connexion enjoyed by Anglicans', the paper's religious correspondent, Clifford Longley, remarked: 'The Bonn Agreement has shown up the weaknesses, as well as the strengths, of the concept of church unity which limits itself to mutual recognition and full communion. While it leaves the identity of each partner undiminished, it cannot generate the sense of a joint collective enterprise. Each partner evolves, as a church, independently of the others, even indifferent to their welfare and self-absorbed.'[30] It would be sad if his words proved true.

On a happier note, Anglicans and Old Catholics have continued to join with each other for worship and occasions of rejoicing. The beautiful chapel of St. Nicholas, Coburg, in Bavaria, dating back to 1473 with some of its medieval mural paintings still preserved, came into Old Catholic possession in the early 1970s after lengthy negotiations. At a solemn Eucharist to celebrate its five hundredth anniversary, presided over by Bishop Brinkhues of Bonn, an Anglican priest representing the Archbishop of Canterbury read out a personal message from him to the congregation.[31] Archbishop Kok took part in the consecration of Eric Kemp 'a very good friend of our churches',[32] and was also present at the enthronement of Donald Coggan as Archbishop of Canterbury. Later that year he visited York Minster where he was to have concelebrated with Stuart Blanch, the Archbishop of York, had not the latter been suddenly taken ill.[33] He was again at Canterbury for Robert Runcie's enthronement in 1979.

The consecration of Professor Glazemaker as Bishop of Deventer at IJmuiden in 1979 was a truly ecumenical event: for, besides having an Anglican and a Roman Catholic bishop present, the new bishop had chosen two friends to hold the bible over his head, one of them an Orthodox priest, and the other a minister of the Dutch Reformed Church. It was perhaps a foretaste of future unity.

On 2 July 1980, the Archbishops of Canterbury and Utrecht concelebrated the Eucharist in Westminster Abbey, a service in which many Old Catholic and Anglican bishops, clergy and laity participated. The sermon preached by Professor Howard Root ended with a plea 'that we jointly consider most seriously and urgently what steps we must now take in the quest of a fuller communion, of *koinonia*'. The service was followed by a lecture given in Church House by the Bishop of Chichester,[34] and a buffet lunch enjoyed by some two hundred and fifty people. It was a worthy celebration of what has been termed the 'model agreement' signed exactly fifty years before.

(b) Independent Churches in Spain, Portugal and the Philippines

Immediately before the opening of the International Old Catholic Congress at Vienna in 1965, an important announcement was made to the delegates present. This was that a concordat of full communion had just been established between the Old Catholic Churches and the Spanish Reformed Episcopal Church, the Lusitanian

Church, Catholic, Apostolic and Evangelical, and the Philippine Independent Church. Its terms were similar to those of the Bonn Agreement of 1931 which, while recognizing local variations in belief and practice, implied that each believed the other to hold all the essentials of the Christian Faith. The three churches concerned had already been granted full communion by the Protestant Episcopal Church of the United States and by the Church of England.

In the case of the first two, each of which had come into existence during the nineteenth century as a protest to certain developments within the Roman Catholic Church, the numbers were small. The Spanish Reformed Episcopal Church had about two thousand members, and the Lusitanian Church about three thousand. Both were originally Evangelical in churchmanship, but by the 1960s had become more liturgically conscious. Their pattern of faith and life, the remarkable tenacity they had demonstrated, and the good standing of their respective bishops, Santos Molina and Luis Pereira, commended them to the churches with which they had already entered into full communion;[35] and this seemed a sufficient guarantee as far as the Old Catholics were concerned.

The third religious body, the Philippine Independent Church, which broke away from Rome and came into being at the beginning of the present century, was far stronger numerically with a membership of about one and a half million. In certain respects during its years of infancy under Bishop Gregorio Aglipay, it resembled the Old Catholic Church: its liturgy was in the vernacular, its clergy were allowed to marry, its lay people were given an important place in church life, and it abandoned what was considered extreme Mariolatry. However, its journey forward was to be an uphill one, with over forty years of waiting before it could win acceptance. After failing in his overtures with Bishop Brent of the American Episcopal Church, Aglipay turned to Bishop Herzog, the head of the Swiss Old Catholics in Berne. At first Herzog was sympathetic, and in a letter to Bishop Brent dated 31 July 1904, wrote: 'It seems to me a duty to render every assistance to the poor Filipinos who are seeking to free themselves from the yoke of Rome and to establish a better order in the ecclesiastical and moral sphere'.[36] But doubts were raised in Bishop Herzog's mind when he heard that Aglipay had not been validly consecrated, and that he and his church were moving towards Unitarianism.

Not until 1946 was the new leader of the Philippine Independent

Church, Isabelo de los Reyes, able to assure the Presiding Bishop of the Protestant Episcopal Church in America that his church was Trinitarian in its belief. Then, together with two other of its bishops, he received consecration according to the Anglican rite at a service held in Manila. Consequently, the Philippine Independent Church was in due course able to enter into full communion with the Protestant Episcopal Church, and later also with the Church of England, the Bonn Agreement once again forming the basis of the concordat.[37] Bishop Isabelo de los Reyes became a highly respected figure among Philippine Christians, and a noted ecumenist. It was fitting that he should have been one of those who, in 1965, signed the concordat establishing communion between his and the Old Catholic Church after a thorough examination by the latter had taken place.

(c) The Orthodox Churches

In the autumn of 1931, a few months after the signing of the agreement with Anglicans, a group of Old Catholic theologians headed by the Archbishop of Utrecht, Francis Kenninck, met at Bonn in conference with representatives of the Orthodox Churches led by the Metropolitan Germanos of Thyateira, Exarch of Western and Central Europe. From the start any hopes of concrete results emerging from this meeting were dashed, when it was learned that while the Old Catholic delegation had full authority to accept the conference's decisions in the name of its church, the Orthodox delegation had no such powers and could only refer the decisions to higher authority. At an early stage in the proceedings the Orthodox raised the question of the *Filioque* clause in the Nicene Creed, and were delighted to be assured that this either had been, or would be, removed from the Old Catholic liturgies. Later on, differences in teaching and practice between the two Churches were discussed. In the final session Dr. Kenninck asked what the Orthodox thought about the Old Catholics, and whether it would be possible for an Ecumenical Council to meet in the future. On the Orthodox side, some of the theologians voiced their desire for intercommunion with Old Catholics but owing to the limitations imposed it was impossible for them to go further.[38]

Dom Clément Lialine reflecting on this meeting has expressed surprise that none of the Orthodox representatives present raised any query concerning the recently concluded concordat between Old

Catholics and Anglicans.[39] Later on, the Bonn Agreement caused the Orthodox serious misgivings, and the Old Catholics found this hard to understand. Archbishop Rinkel, speaking at a reception arranged by the Society of St. Willibrord in London in 1937, said that to the Old Catholic mind there was no question either of theology, ethics, faith or order which should prevent immediate intercommunion between the Eastern Churches on the one hand, and the Anglican and Old Catholic Churches on the other.

Further discussions came to a halt with the outbreak of World War II. Immediately peace was restored, letters were exchanged between the Archbishop of Utrecht and the Metropolitan of Thyateira, Archbishop Germanos. The latter began: 'Great is our God, who through sufferings and trials has preserved to this day our peoples and ourselves and bestows upon us his grace and courage to continue our work for the prevalence of his kingdom on earth: praised be his name always and from the ages to the ages. Amen.' He went on to say that he would be very glad to avail himself of the first opportunity to meet, and to renew the old friendship existing between their two Churches.[40]

It was due to the initiative of Archbishop Germanos that at the International Old Catholic Congress held at Hilversum in 1948, a delegation from the Russian Orthodox Theological Institute in Paris was present. One of its members, after listening to a paper by Professor Urs Küry of Switzerland on 'The General Theological Foundations of Ecumenical Reconstruction' was moved to declare that no doctrinal barrier existed to prevent union between the Orthodox and Old Catholic Churches.

Among the Orthodox representatives attending the International Old Catholic Congress at Rheinfelden in 1957 was one who came on behalf of the Patriarchate of Moscow, and who received a special welcome from members of the Congress. The proceedings at Rheinfelden included a paper by a prominent Old Catholic layman, Berthold Spüler, on the current situation in the Orthodox Churches. Dr. Spüler, a professor of the University of Hamburg, through his informative articles contributed to the *IKZ* over a period of many years, has perhaps done more than anyone to maintain the interest of Old Catholics in Orthodox affairs.

The most important paper delivered at the International Old Catholic Congress at Haarlem in 1961 was that of Archbishop Rinkel on 'Old Catholics and Orthodox', in which he maintained that in his opinion there were no doctrinal barriers between the two churches. They shared the same faith, tradition, Scriptures and Creeds, as well as the teaching of the Fathers and Ecumenical Councils; they had the same Sacraments and the same Apostolic Ministry of bishops, priests and deacons. He stressed that in their own belief and intention Old Catholics accepted the Orthodox faith in its fullness, and that they longed for the day when they could enjoy full communion with their Orthodox brethren. His plea for unity was enforced by the emphasis laid by Michael Ramsey in his address at the theological conference before the Congress, on the need for Anglicans and Old Catholics to work together for unity with the Orthodox Churches.

A more promising outlook for the future stemmed from the third Pan-Orthodox Conference which was held at Rhodes in 1964 and decided upon:

(1) The immediate formation of an Inter-Orthodox Theological Commission composed of theological specialists, the number and names to be announced later;

(2) The systematic preparation by this Commission of the Orthodox theses for the future theological discussion on the basis of the doctrinal, dogmatic and liturgical texts of the Old Catholic Church;

(3) The commencement of the discussions with the corresponding Theological Commission of the Old Catholic Church, after mutual consultation between the two Churches.[41]

Professor Werner Küppers returned from the Pan-Orthodox Conference filled with enthusiasm. In his later years he worked hard to promote deeper understanding with the Orthodox, speaking frequently on the subject and contributing articles on 'Orthodox-altkatholisher Dialog' to the *IKZ*.

Nevertheless, it appears that some Old Catholics were beginning to feel a sense of frustration at the Orthodox attitude. As the result of discussions during his visit to Sofia and Belgrade in the autumn of 1968, Dr. Urs Küry, the Bishop in Berne and a distinguished Old Catholic scholar, prepared a memorandum for the leaders of the Bulgarian and Serbian Orthodox Churches. After briefly outlining the developments in Orthodox and Old Catholic conversations since 1931, Bishop Küry was constrained to remark that while the Bonn Agreement had given the Orthodox food for earnest thought, it had sometimes led to sheer prejudice on their part. The Old Catholics were, he claimed, now reproached for their intercommunion with

Anglicans, just as they had previously been for the *Filioque* clause in the Creed, and for their Eucharistic teaching and their orders. The most recent manifestation of this had been at the 1966 Orthodox Theological Conference in Bulgaria, where objections were raised which the Old Catholics supposed had been long overcome. Press reports of that conference were a bitter disappointment for the Old Catholics. In view of this, Dr. Küry expressed on behalf of himself and his fellow-bishops the wish that the Orthodox and Old Catholic theological commissions should arrange a joint meeting as soon as possible, in order that they might become bettter informed about each other.[42]

When representative Orthodox and Old Catholic theologians met together at Chambesy, near Geneva, in the autumn of 1970, agreement was reached on some points where this had previously been lacking. Other differences of opinion which existed did not seem to be real barriers to unity. Notwithstanding this, it was clear that the intercommunion between the Old Catholics and Anglicans presented problems for the Orthodox, particularly in view of the proposed Anglican-Methodist scheme.[43] If one looks back to a study on the relations between Orthodox and Old Catholics by Professor Karmiris of Athens in the *IKZ* of 1950, there will be evident a note of regret that these had not borne the fruit which had earlier been expected. The Orthodox took the view that this was due to Protestant influences on the Old Catholics. In his article in the same journal some twenty-two years later,[44] Professor Küppers was even more outspoken, giving the warning of 'a thunder-cloud on the horizon'.[45] Old Catholics were now left in no doubt that before they and the Orthodox could really come together in any spiritual co-operation, there had to be come clarification of the 1931 Bonn Agreement with Anglicans, and of the 1965 concordat with the Episcopal Churches of Spain and Portugal and the Independent Church of the Philippines. The reason given by the Orthodox was that these churches with which the Old Catholics had entered into communion also had relations with other Protestant groups and churches: a factor which could well prove an insuperable obstacle to unity as far as the Orthodox were concerned.

In the light of these reflections it will be understood why Old Catholics, who have a deep longing for union with their brethren of Eastern Christendom, should view with misgivings the recent trends on the part of some Anglicans already mentioned.

(d) The Roman Catholic Church

For more than thirty years after the Bonn Agreement with Anglicans had been reached, Old Catholics remained aloof from their brethren of the Roman Communion. In fact, the proclamation by Pope Pius XII in 1950 of the dogma of Mary's bodily Assumption served to created a further barrier: for in a statement signed by Archbishop Rinkel and Bishop Küry on behalf of the Churches united through the Declaration of Utrecht, this dogma was emphatically rejected by Old Catholics.

However, with the advent of Pope John XXIII and the Second Vatican Council a change took place. Fr. Victor Conzemius, a Roman Catholic scholar and good friend of the Old Catholics, has drawn attention to a number of currents which had for many years been present in the Old Catholic Church and now found a place on the agenda of the Vatican Council. These were:

(1) The introduction of the vernacular into the liturgy;
(2) The encouragement of an active participation by the laity in Church life;
(3) The renewal of episcopal collegiality;
(4) The concern for Christian unity.[46]

These striking parallels between the revival within Roman Catholicism and what had already been realized by the Old Catholics certainly helped to pave the way for a new understanding between the two churches. The Dean of the Metropolitan Chapter of Utrecht, Dr. P. J. Maan, was invited to be an observer for all the Churches belonging to the Union of Utrecht at Vatican II, and he officiated with Pope Paul VI in one of the services at the closing of the Council. A move forward on Rome's part was to send Fr. Conzemius as an official observer at the 1965 International Old Catholic Congress in Vienna. Welcoming him, the Old Catholic president commented that while the first two of such Congresses held at Vienna in 1897 and 1909 had been dominated by the polemic against Rome, and the third Congress at Vienna in 1931 had displayed interest in the Ecumenical Movement, the present one was marked by the complete disappearance of anti-Roman feelings.

Yet there still remained a long-standing refusal on the Roman side to enter into any dialogue with Old Catholics until the latter subscribed to the 'Formulary of Alexander VII' of 1665 condemning Jansenism, and to Clement XI's bull 'Unigenitus' of 1713 pronouncing sentence against Paschasius Quesnel's book *Moral Reflections on the New Testmaent*. A group of Dutch Old Catholic and Roman Catholic theologians now re-examined this question and arrived at the conclusion that the time had come when an obligation which had been laid down in circumstances entirely different from the present, ought to be annulled. A joint request for this to be done was sent to Cardinal Bea, head of the Vatican Secretariat for promoting Christian Unity, and Cardinal Alfrink, the Roman Catholic Archbishop of Utrecht addressed him a letter in similar terms. In due course Pope Paul VI gave his consent to the request, and in March 1966 Cardinal Alfrink was officially informed that Old Catholics need no longer subscribe to the documents before dialogue between the two churches could begin.

Accordingly, on the following St. Willibrord's day, 7 November, an historic ceremony took place in St. Gertrude's Cathedral, Utrecht in the form of a joint act of worship shared by both Archbishop Rinkel and Cardinal Alfrink. In addition there were present seven Dutch Old Catholic and Roman Catholic bishops, as well as four Old Catholic bishops from Switzerland and Germany. The Reverend David Tustin also attended as representative of the Archbishop of Canterbury. When the moment arrived for the two archbishops to address the assembly, Cardinal Alfrink spoke first. He described the ceremony as a milestone and resting-place: the end of one era and the beginning of another. At the same time, he pointed out that what had been achieved that evening would have little meaning unless both churches grew closer together in the process of *rapprochement*. Archbishop Rinkel, in an excellent speech, called for courage to tread the new path; and he announced that the members of the joint working party would be nominated as the official committee for dialogue, which could start at once. Finally, both archbishops stood side by side at the altar and simultaneously intoned the blessing, bringing a memorable service to its conclusion. As the recessional hymn – a Dutch translation of the traditional Latin hymn of St. Willibrord – ended, and the two archbishops moved out of sight, the large congregation broke into a spontaneous outburst of applause.[47]

In the sober aftermath of this exciting event, it gradually dawned that what had taken place was only a modest beginning. Obstacles like the questions of papal infallibility and primacy were still to be overcome, and there would have to be much hard discussion ahead. Nevertheless, there were obvious signs of a new spirit abroad at the time when Marinus Kok was elected Bishop-Coadjutor of the Old Catholic archdiocese of Utrecht in 1969. News of the election and forthcoming consecration was despatched as usual to the Vatican; but whereas in the past such information had met with a sharp rebuff, on this occasion Pope Paul VI sent the new bishop a personal letter of congratulations.[48] The Roman Catholic Church was represented at the consecration by the Bishop of Groningen who sat in the sanctuary; some Dutch members of the Roman Communion present thought he should have taken part in the laying-on of hands!

The theme of the International Old Catholic Theologians' Conference, held at Zurich in the autumn of 1969, was 'The Roman Catholic – Old Catholic Dialogue'. It was yet another indication of the happier relations between the two churches that the conference took place in a recently opened Roman Catholic academy, with its chapel, vestments and communion vessels being used for the daily Eucharist. Canon Eric Kemp, the Anglican representative at the conference, formed the opinion that the Old Catholic attitudes towards Rome were somewhat coloured by the state of the Roman Catholic Church in the country to which they belonged. For example, Professor Naumczyk from Warsaw was emphatic that Vatican II had had little influence in Poland, and that there was no prospect of any dialogue between the Polish Catholic Church and Rome, at least as long as Cardinal Wyszynski remained in control. In Holland, on the other hand, there were close relations everywhere, and in Rotterdam the Roman Catholics shared an Old Catholic church, and both used the same Reserved Sacrament. Eric Kemp was impressed by the high level of the papers and discussions at the conference. He noted Archbishop Rinkel's praise for the writings of William Temple, and his comment that Anglican theologians had much to contribute to the subjects being discussed. He was particularly struck by the Germans who were present, and felt that under the leadership of Bishop Brinkhues of Bonn, the Old Catholics in Germany had a very hopeful future.[49]

Already, official conversations had opened between Bishop Urs Küry, the Old Catholic Bishop of Berne, and Bishop Charrière of Fribourg the spokesman of the Roman Catholic bishops of Switzerland for ecumenical relations, and a discussion group had been established with the object of getting rid of old misunderstandings, and of promoting joint witness and action. Bishop Küry in his memorandum to the Orthodox bishops of Belgrade and Serbia, to which reference has already been made, stressed the desire of the Old Catholics to meet the Orthodox 'to give more exact information about our relations with the Roman Catholic Church which have entered a new phase'.[50] In Germany, in 1970, Bishop Brinkhues and Cardinal Lorenz Jäger met in conference with the theologians of the committee for mutual conversations. There was complete agreement on sacramental teaching, and on Scripture and tradition as sources of revelation; and although the Old Catholics were unable to accept papal infallibility, they recognized the historic primacy of honour which various ecumenical Councils had accorded the Bishop of Rome. It was therefore felt that the initial aim of a *rapprochement* between the two Churches should be a partial intercommunion with admission to each other's sacraments.[51]

In the autumn of 1972, Archbishop Kok informed Dr. Ramsey that, as the result of recent negotiations, the International Bishops' Conference of the Union of Utrecht and the Secretariat for Promoting Christian Unity in Rome had accepted the so-called *Züricher Nota* as a base for making practical arrangements to work as Christians together in a limited communion. He emphasized that this agreement would in no way affect that which already existed between Old Catholics and Anglicans. On the contrary, he hoped the new understanding with the Roman Catholic Church would help in fostering good relations between Anglicans and Roman Catholics.[52] Michael Ramsey replied: 'How warmly I welcome this news and I pray that this further drawing together of divided Christians will bring nearer the day when all men will be one in Christ our Lord.'[53]

As the year 1981 drew to its close, news came that the Roman Catholic Archbishop of Utrecht, Cardinal Willebrands, had signed an agreement with Archbishop Kok for intercommunion, and that similar steps had been taken between the Roman Catholic and Old Catholic leaders in Germany and Switzerland. It should therefore be possible to implement the *Züricher Nota* in the immediate future, thus moving forward another step towards the ultimate goal.

On Sunday 13 September 1981, Marinus Kok celebrated the fortieth anniversary of his ordination to the priesthood with a Eucharist in his cathedral, at which there were some four hundred communicants. It was a happy occasion, and afterwards a letter of congratulations from the Archbishop of Canterbury, Robert Runcie, was handed to him.[54] This was followed by the presentation of gifts from his people, and an enthusiastic demonstration of affection by the children for both the archbishop and Mrs. Kok. Less than two months later Dr. Runcie paid a visit to Utrecht and shared with its archbishop in a great service for St. Willibrord's day at St. Gertrude's Cathedral, a building which has featured so prominently in the events of the past fifty years.

The time had now arrived when Archbishop Kok felt it right to lay down the heavy burden of office. His successor – Mgr. Glazemaker – yet another in the long line going back to St. Willibrord – will have the task of guiding the Old Catholic Churches along the path ahead. May he be filled with the charity which 'will continue to push us forward to our Lord's ideal of one flock with one Shepherd'.[55]

NOTES

1. R. Rouse and S. C. Neill (eds.), *A History of the Ecumenical Movement 1517–1948* (1954), p. 635.
2. ibid., pp. 470–1.
3. Archives of the Archbishops of Utrecht, Utrecht (hereafter *AAU*), 28 Sept. 1931.
4. *AAU*, Lang to Kenninck, 29 Jan. 1932.
5. *AAU*, Rinkel to Ed. Flannery Jr., 2 Jan. 1960.
6. *Church Times* 23 Sept. 1954.
7. ibid.
8. *AAU*, 21 Oct. 1954.
9. Patrick C. Rodger, 'Letter from Geneva' in *Theology*, June 1963, pp. 229–33.
10. Gordon Huelin, *St. Willibrord and His Society*, p. 69.
11. *Church Times* 30 Nov. 1945, *Confirmation in a Dutch Church at the Hague*.
12. *AAU*, 14 April 1945.
13. *AAU*, Rinkel to Headlam, 4 Aug. 1945.
14. *AAU*, T. W. Freeman to Rinkel, 24 Feb. 1946.
15. *AAU*, Rinkel to Freeman, 3 Apr. 1946.
16. *AAU*, C. B. Moss to Rinkel, 26 Oct. 1950.
17. Counsellors on Foreign Relations/Old Catholic files (hereafter *CFR/OC*), Lambeth Palace, Report on fifteenth International Old Catholic Congress at Hilversum, 17–21 Aug. 1948.
18. *Saint Willibrord News* Sept. 1981.
19. C. B. Moss, 'Twenty five Years of Union with the Old Catholic Churches', *Church Times*, 9 Aug. 1957.

20. L. Gauthier, 'Pour le 25e anniversaire de l'intercommunion anglicane et vielle-catholique', *IKZ*, 1956, pp. 133–49.
21. *CFR/OC* Report by Kenneth Riches 7 Oct. 1957.
22. *AAU*, Rinkel to Scaife, 13 June 1961.
23. V. Conzemius, 'Le XIXe Congrès International des Vieux-Catholiques à Vienne' *Irénikon* 38 (1965), p. 465.
24. *CFR/OC* J. A. Burley to J. R. Satterthwaite, 22 Apr. 1969 and Rinkel to Ramsey, 9 May 1969.
25. *CFR/OC* Ramsey to Rinkel, 13 May 1969.
26. *AAU*, Yashiro to Rinkel, 20 Aug. 1962.
27. *AAU*, Kok to Kemp, 29 May 1974.
28. *AAU*, Kok to Ramsey, 26 Apr. 1972.
29. *AAU*, Kok to Ramsey, 29 Mar. 1974.
30. *Times* 29 June 1981.
31. This was the Revd. Ernest Gordon who kindly supplied these details.
32. *AAU*, Kok to Ramsey, 15 Aug. 1974.
33. The Bishop of Selby concelebrated in place of Blanch.
34. A précis is contained in Appendix II.
35. *The Luisitanian Church Catholic, Apostolic, Evangelical and the Spanish Reformed Episcopal Church: A Report of the Commission appointed by the Archbishop of Canterbury to examine the Faith and Order of these Churches* (1963). Both these Churches became fully part of the Anglican Communion in 1980.
36. P. S. de Achútegui and M. A. Bernad, *Religious revolution in the Philippines. The life and church of Gregorio Aglipay 1860–1960* (2nd. ed. 1961), p. 395.
37. L. B. Whittemore, *Struggle for Freedom* (1961), p. 217.
38. 'Relations between the Orthodox and Old Catholic Churches' *Christian East* (spring 1932), pp. 91–8.
39. C. Lialine, 'Vieux-catholiques et Orthodoxes en quête d'union', *Istina*, 5 (1958), pp. 22–56.
40. *AAU*, Germanos to Rinkel, 16 Oct. 1945.
41. *One in Christ*, I, 2 (1965), p. 152.
42. *CFR/OC* Memorandum for his Beatitude Patriarch Kyril and the Holy Synod of the Bulgarian Orthodox Church and his Beatitude German and the Holy Synod and the Theological Faculty of the Serbian Orthodox Church, Oct. 1968.
43. *CFR/OC* Extract from *Christkatolisches Kirkenblatt*, 21 Aug. 1971.
44. W. Küppers, *Stand und Perspektiven des altkatholisch-orthodoxen Dialogs, IKZ*, 1972, pp. 87–114.
45. ibid., p. 104.
46. V. Conzemius, 'Catholicism, Old and Roman,' *Journal of Ecumenical Studies* 4 (1967), pp. 426–46. I am indebted to Fr. Conzemius tor sending me a copy of his important and fuller study, *Katholizismus ohne Rom.*
47. *CFR/OC* Report by David Tustin 10 Nov. 1966.

48. *Church Times* 2 Jan. 1970.
49. *CFR/OC* Report by Eric Kemp 28 Sept. 1968.
50. see note 41 above.
51. *CFR/OC* Report of joint conference between Cardinal Jager and Bishop Brinkhues.
52. *CFR/OC* Kok to Ramsey, 9 Oct. 1972.
53. *CFR/OC* Ramsey to Kok, 20 Oct. 1972.
54. I was privileged to be present and to be the bearer of both the letter and verbal greetings.
55. The closing words of Archbishop Kok's sermon on St. Willibrord's day, 7 Nov. 1981.

Appendix I

The Bonn Agreement 1931

Statement agreed between the representatives of the Old Catholic Churches and the Churches of the Anglican Communion at a Conference held at Bonn

JULY 2, 1931

1. Each Communion recognizes the catholicity and independence of the other and maintains its own.

2. Each Communion agrees to admit members of the other Communion to participate in the Sacraments.

3. Intercommunion does not require from either Communion the acceptance of all doctrinal opinion, sacramental devotion, or liturgical practice characteristic of the other, but implies that each believes the other to hold all the essentials of the Christian Faith.

Signed:

A. C. GLOUCESTER:	G. F. GRAHAM-BROWN.
[A. C. Headlam]	C. B. MOSS.
STAUNTON FULHAM.	C. L. GAGE-BROWN.
[B. S. Batty]	J. H. DEVENTER.
A. S. DUNCAN-JONES.	ADOLF KÜRY.
N. P. WILLIAMS.	GEORG MOOG.
J. A. DOUGLAS.	A. RINKEL.

Appendix II

Précis of a Lecture by the Right Reverend Eric Kemp, Bishop of Chichester, 2 July 1981

Today is the exact fiftieth anniversary of the Bonn Agreement between Anglicans and Old Catholics. Intercommunion was achieved not by the Bonn statement itself, but by the exchange of resolutions of the respective synods between the Archbishops of Canterbury and Utrecht. Other provinces severally ratified these resolutions in later months and years. Intercommunion gained visible expression as Old Catholic bishops partook in the consecrations of two Anglican bishops in 1932. Significantly, intercommunion did not require of either Communion 'acceptance of all doctrinal opinion, sacramental devotion or liturgical practice' of the other. It implied mutual belief in all the 'essentials of the Christian faith'.

J. M. Neale's *History of the so-called Jansenist Church of Holland* (1858) first drew Anglican attention to Old Catholicism. It related the causes of the Dutch schism, the consecration of Archbishop Steenoven in 1723, and subsequent reunion attempts. The dominant issue was that of authority, in two distinct forms related to the First Vatican Council.

One was the papal claim to universal jurisdiction. Not now emphasized by Rome, that claim in the 17th and 18th centuries included power to suppress and control national churches such as the Dutch. It justified the appointment of an archbishop of Utrecht being postponed from 1710 to 1723, and the frustration of subsequent reunion endeavours. The consecration of Steenoven epitomized Dutch opposition to papal powers, reflected much later in the 'Declaration on Primacy in the Church' (1970), which reiterates the doctrine of Saint Gregory the Great. Papal authority remains a core issue between Rome and all other churches.

The second problem concerned papal infallibility. Gaspari's Catechism, typical of Roman doctrine just prior to the Second Vatican Council, gives papal infallibility prominence in a wide variety of peripheral teaching. Refusal to accept this merited severe discipline. In 1827, Archbishop van Santen was required by a papal nuncio to affirm that five Jansenist Propositions, condemned in the Bulls *Cum occasione* (1653) and *Unigenitus* (1713), occurred in Jansen's *Augustinus* (itself condemned by Pope Urban VII). Van Santen had simply to admit disobedience, to acknowledge the heresy, and 'to silence all trifling scruples'.

Our contemporary problem is the infallibility question itself, and also its tendency to repress historical examination and revision. The Bull *Apostolicae Curae* is of special significance to Anglicans in this respect, as an obstacle to relations with Rome.

Old Catholic history began with the excommunication of the Dutch Church, and proceeded through a second phase in which the decrees of the First Vatican Council were contested, and the Union of Utrecht formed.

Completion of work by the Anglican Roman Catholic International Commission is important owing to its view of the Roman ethos. The question of Authority, probed at Trier in 1980, must be examined further, to provide a working text for debate with Utrecht and Rome.

It should be emphasized that (as Bishop Swayne of Lincoln said in 1932) intercommunion is union. Degrees of union were envisaged by Archbishop Fisher, and subsequently by sundry ecumenical bodies, but what is now termed 'Full Communion' is of necessity somewhat anomalous. A sacramental relationship goes far beyond the simple mutual reception of Holy Communion, and worship at a common altar. The Liturgical Movement has shown that sharing the Eucharist entails a life of common concerns. It reaches into decisions on faith and morals, and places a limitation on freedom of selfish action.

Anglicans and Old Catholics have enjoyed participating together in conferences and congresses, occasionally prompted by the Society of Saint Willibrord and other agencies, but both sides have been slow to recognize the limits imposed by union. The Anglican Consultative Council has failed singularly in this respect. Anglican, Orthodox and Old Catholic dialogue should be related more closely.

Sadly, relations have been strained. Old Catholics resented the lack of consultation in the 1950s about the South India reunion scheme. Though dialogue has occurred over the Anglican-Methodist proposals, and in the question of the ordination of women, opinions vary about the propriety of unilateral action by any historic episcopalian church. Consequently, the Polish National Catholic Church suspended communion with the Episcopal Church. Realization of the present Covenant Proposals could significantly endanger relations between Canterbury and Utrecht.

Are ambiguities in the third clause of the Bonn Agreement now proving awkward? Late in 1931, Archbishop Kenninck reiterated in a letter the second and third principles of the Bonn Agreement. It may now be significant however, that instead of the first, he wrote about the recognition of the validity of Anglican ordinations, even though such recognition had already been assured in 1925. Anglicans had never questioned Old Catholic orders, despite their occasional departure from Nicene requirement of three episcopal consecrators. But, as Pope Leo XIII had judged against Anglican orders, Old Catholic recognition was necessary to any subsequent discussion. Thus Old Catholics and Anglicans did not differ in their attitudes to apostolic ministry, as Anglicans did with Free Churches or with Rome. Old Catholic participation in Anglican consecrations was never viewed as a method of validation.

Thus the third clause of the Bonn Agreement, though cautious, cannot cover serious theological or practical differences relating to ordination. If an Anglican province departs from the 1931 conditions, Old Catholics are entitled to see this as a unilateral departure, modifying their commitment to intercommunion. The Utrecht position is that 'We must not make any more schisms'. Adverse Anglican decisions may limit the intercommunion enjoyed so far for fifty years.

Our problems are caused by failure to share worship and consult theologically, particularly about apostolic ministry and episcopal authority. What is the nature of the episcopal college and its relationship to the local churches? Such matters require urgent and lengthy consultation. Moreover, we require a real sense of partnership in the Church's mission, relating Christ to the world and to our time, rather than confining it to its traditional European setting.

Anglicans and Old Catholics together have an important contribution to make to the solution of the pressing world problems of our time. May these Jubilee celebrations strengthen our wills to co-operate in the discovery of a diversity in unity making for a true witness to the Gospel.

Appendix III

The Hymnology of the Old Catholic Church as a Reflection of its Self-comprehension

1. 'Lex orandi – lex credendi' was the basic principle of the ancient Church. This means that the depth of one's faith can be recognized by the way in which one prays.

When after 1723 the Church of Utrecht claimed the ancient right of electing its own bishops independently of Rome and thereby, from Rome's point of view, destroyed the communion with the Holy See, it laid great stress on its recognition as the 'Roman Catholic Church of the Old Episcopal Clergy.'

This ecclesiological understanding of itself was also expressed by the retention of the post Tridentine Roman liturgy in all its details, and it was only in 1909 that the common language of the people was permitted for the celebration of the Holy Eucharist. This meant also that the musical forms of the Latin Mass were decisive for church services. Even after the introduction of the Dutch language in the Eucharist the liturgical hymns of the 'Proper' and the 'Ordinarium' of the Mass were retained. Andreas Rinkel, later archbishop, set a large number of such liturgical texts to music, which congregations of the Old Catholic Church of the Netherlands still enjoy singing.

2. The development in the German-speaking Old Catholic Churches was quite different, as a result of different spiritual prerequisites. In the Catholicism of the years between 1800 and 1870 there were already more than five hundred hymnbooks with German settings of the Mass and other hymns. The founder of Old Catholic liturgical reform in Germany and Switzerland, Prof. Dr. Adolf Thürlings (1844–1915) remarks 'that this flood spreads with an impetuosity, which would shock Rome if anyone there had an idea of it'.

This development betrays a growing understanding of itself by the church, that did not grow out of a centrally governed and uniform church but emphasized the uniqueness, the spiritual experiences and expressions of Pietism of the various 'local churches' (as we today generally say in ecumenical theology). Thus there was an understanding of itself identical to that of the ancient church, even if here and there it was not fully conscious.

It is therefore not surprising that the protest against the 'new' Papal dogmas of 1870, which appealed to the ideas of the ancient church, were closely connected with these movements and forms of pietism. In addition

Roman centralism rejected the individual developments and sought to hinder them by strict measures. Thus one of the leading reformers, H. Ignaz von Wessenberg, episcopal administrator of Constance was not consecrated bishop. Indeed, the honourable see of Constance was after a thousand years of existence dissolved without any thought of the consequences.

3. The dogmatic development which was to lead to the Papal dogmas of 1870 had a parallel, which is too little known and has been too little researched: a liturgical restoration movement in the Catholic Church brought in the second half of the nineteenth century the 'more continuing alignment with Rome than had ever before existed'. 'Along with grievances from the Age of Enlightenment centuries-old partly ecclesiastical customs . . . were disputed with regard to their legality and discontinued'. That is how the Roman Catholic Liturgy expert Prof. Dr. Philipp Harnoncourt of Graz described it recently.

On the other hand the history of hymns in the mother tongue had had a long history in Germany and Switzerland, the cradle of the Reformation. In addition the spiritual movement of Protestant hymnology brought a rich tradition of hymns into the Catholic dioceses of areas where the denominations were mixed.

This was where the attitude we now call 'ecumenical' began to be discussed in the nineteenth century. Ernst Moritz Arndt wrote in 1819 demanding a hymnbook 'for all Christians, without differing between special denominations and individual attitudes, without considering this or that denomination'.

We can now determine two basic ideas in the Old Catholic movement which developed after 1870. First and foremost the adherents of the movement retained their identity with pre-1870 Catholicism, and insisted on continuing to possess unchanged all the privileges and duties of Catholic Christians. On the other hand Rome's excommunication and the ensuing development of autonomy led congregations and dioceses to a greater freedom. Thus they were able to retain and continue the independent developments which Rome had fought against.

It is not surprising that in Germany alone between 1875 and the Second World War the publication of about thirty Old Catholic hymnbooks can be identified. About ten similar publications existed before the appearance in 1893 of a newly-issued *Hymnbook of the Christian Catholic Church of Switzerland*, which was re-issued unchanged numerous times.

4. The ecumenical openmindedness of early Old Catholicism, which had already led to the so-called 'Bonn Union Conferences' of 1874 and 1875, was to be seen also in church singing. The hymnbooks not only continued the handing down of Catholic hymns in the German language, but also increasingly took over Reformation hymns. This is particularly the case in the *Hymnbook of the Kingdom of God*, published in 1885 by Adolf Thürlings. The way this was used shows the importance of this development.

In Catholic liturgy hymns in the mother tongue played a minor rôle. They could be used only in addition to the actual liturgical texts, which had to be sung or prayed by the priest and by the choir. It was held to be a rather liberal practice if, for example, the priest prayed the actual Mass texts silently while the congregation sang a hymn at the same time.

The Old Catholic Church wanted to go a stage further (which only happened in the Roman Catholic Church after the Second Vatican Council!) and give the hymn the position it already had in the Reformed Churches, and not even yet in the Anglican Church. It was – as Thürlings put it – 'to be used as a substitute for certain parts of the liturgy; in such a case however it is not to be used freely parallel to the liturgy led by the priest, but must fit into the latter in the same way as the text it has replaced'. This results of course in a high demand from the texts and melodies of the hymns, which are no longer an expression of individual pietism but of the official liturgy of the church.

The consequence of this was that now for the first time Protestant hymns became an integral part of Catholic Liturgy.

This open avowal of the spiritual communion of the whole of Christendom led for a long time to the accusation that Old Catholicism was in reality 'New Protestantism', a thesis particularly upheld by Conrad Gröber, Archbishop of Freiburg, in his *Handbook of Religious Questions of Today*, published in 1937.

The Second Vatican Council was to show that Roman Catholic Liturgical Reform had to follow the Old Catholic Church along these lines.

5. It was therefore only consistent that the Old Catholic Church of the German-speaking areas should join the 'Working Committee for Ecumenical Hymnody', founded in 1969, and declare itself prepared to adapt the use of the ecumenical common texts and melodies. The Old Catholic Church in the Netherlands has more recently taken similar steps.

Thus is revealed in the history of Old Catholic Hymnody the church's understanding of itself: The Old Catholics regard themselves as a Catholic Church. They treasure the freedom and the individual spirituality of the 'local churches' and reject all attempts at central direction. They know that the Spirit of God works in all Christian churches, and they are ready to adapt as their own the spiritual fruits of other churches.

6. It is, however, surprising that there has not, even since 1931, been a closer connection with Anglican hymnody. Only in a few individual cases have German and English hymns been sung or texts in both languages been set to common melodies in joint Old Catholic/Anglican services. Even the recently published new hymnal of the Christian Catholic Church of Switzerland (1978) displays this lack. Here is a field of opportunity for our common future.

Select Bibliography

Manuscript Material

Archives of the Archbishops of Utrecht
Old Catholic Files of the Archbishop's Counsellors on Foreign Relations,
Lambeth Palace, London
St. Willibrord Society Minute Books

Journals etc.

Anglican Theological Review
Christkatholischer Hauskalender
Chronicle of the Convocation of Canterbury
Church Times
Ecumenical Bulletin (of the Episcopal Church of the U.S.A.)
Internationale Kirchliche Zeitschrift
Kirchliches Jahrbuch für die Alt-Katholiken in Deutschland
PNCC Studies
Saint Willibrord News

Printed Sources

ACHÚTEGUI, P. S. De and BERNAD, M. A., *Religious revolution in the Philippines: The life and church of Gregorio Aglipay, 1860–1960* (2nd. ed.), Manila, 1961
ANDREWS, T., *The Polish National Catholic Church in America and Poland*, London, 1953
Archbishop of Canterbury's Commission Report, *The Lusitanian Church, Catholic, Apostolic, Evangelical, and the Spanish Reformed Episcopal Church*, London, 1963
ARNDT, E. M., *Von dem Wort und dem Kirchliede* (reprint), Hildesheim, 1970
BARNARD, L. W., *C. B. Moss, 1888–1964*, London, 1967
BELL, G. K. A., *Randall Davidson* (ch. LXIII 'The case of Bishop Mathew'), London, 1935
CONZEMIUS, V., *Katholizismus ohne Rom*, Zurich-Einsiedeln-Cologne, 1969
FOX, P., *The Polish National Catholic Church*, Scranton, 1956
HARNONCOURT, P., *Gesamtkirchliche und teilkirchliche Liturgie*, Freiburg-Basle-Vienna, 1974
HUELIN, G., *Saint Willibrord and His Society*, London, 1960
JANOWSKI, R., *The Growth of a Church*, Scranton, 1965

KEMP, E. W., *The Church of England and the Old Catholic Churches*, in E. G. W. Bill (ed.), *Anglican initiatives in Christian unity* (pp. 145–62), London, 1967

KLEEF, B. A. van, *Geschiedenis van de Oud-katholieke Kerk van Nederland*, Assen, 1953

KRAFT, S., *Der deutsche Gemeindegesang in der alt-katholischen Kirche* Berne and Karlsruhe, 1976

KÜRY, U., *Die Altkatholische Kirche* (2nd. ed.), Stuttgart, 1978

MOSS, C. B., *The Old Catholic Movement* (2nd ed.), London, 1964

NEALE, J. M., *A History of the so-called Jansenist Church of Holland*, London, 1858

PETERKIEWICZ, J., *The Third Adam*, London, 1975

ROUSE, R. and NEILL, S. C. (eds.), *A History of the Ecumenical Movement 1517–1948*, London, 1954

Society of St. Willibrord, *Eucharistic Worship – Old Catholic Church of the Netherlands* (n. d.)

STEPHENSON, A., *Anglicans and the Lambeth Conferences*, London, 1978

SYKES, S., *The Integrity of Anglicanism*, London, 1978

THÜRLINGS, A., *Leiderbuch vom Reiche Gottes*, Mannheim, 1885

THÜRLINGS, A., *Wie entstehen Kirchengesänge?*, Leipzig, 1907

WHITTEMORE, L. B., *Struggle for Freedom. History of the Philippine Independent Church*, Greenwich, Con., 1961

WLODARSKI, S., *The Origin and Growth of the Polish National Catholic Church*, Scranton, 1974

WRIGHT, J. R. (ed.), *A Communion of Communions: One Eucharistic Fellowship*, New York, 1979

Index